Quit Smoking & Alcohol Hypnosis (2 In 1): Guided Self-Hypnosis & Meditations To Overcome Alcoholism & Smoking Cessation Including Positive Affirmations & Visualizations

By Meditation Made Effortless

Quit Smoking Hypnosis: Guided Self-Hypnosis & Meditations To Stop Smoking Addiction & Smoking Cessation Including Positive Affirmations, Visualizations & Relaxation Techniques

By Meditation Made Effortless

Copyright © 2020

All rights reserved.
No material in this book is to be utilized, reproduced in any electronic form, including recording, photocopying without permission from the author.

Table of Contents

Introduction 1
Induction 2
Deepener 4
Be a Non-Smoker Script 5
Deep Relaxation Script 7
Inner Child Healing 9
Increased Self Confidence 11
Light the Fire Within – Empowering Yourself 13
Quit Smoking Confidence 17
Stop Smoking Script 19
Smoking Pros and Cons 22
Road to Stopping Smoking 24
Keep the Motivation Going 27
Smoking Cessation 29
Appreciate Yourself 31
Sleep Better 33
Stop smoking II 36
White Light Meditation 42
Sleep Reprogramming 45
Stop Smoking with Self Hypnosis 48
The Time Distortion Method 52
Learning to Relax 55
Smoking Cessation II 60
Hypnosis Benefits Script 63
Silky Breathing 66
Staying Committed Script 69
Get rid of the Compulsion Script 73
Live a Smoke Free Life 76
Affirmations 78

To the Narrator

The Introduction, Induction, and Deepener should be 45 Min Long
Be a Non Smoker should be 15 Min Long
Deep Relaxation should be 20 Min Long
Inner Child Healing should be 15 Min Long
Increased Self Confidence should be 20 min long
Light the Fire Within should be 20 min long
Quit Smoking Confidence should be 20 min long
Stop Smoking I should be 15 min long
Smoking Pros and Cons should be 25 min long
Road to Stop Smoking should be 20 min long
Keep the Motivation Going should be 20 min long
Smoking Cessation I should be 20 min long
Appreciate Yourself should be 20min long
Stop Smoking II should be 20 min long
Sleep Reprogramming should be 40 min long
White Light Meditation should be 20 min long
Stop Smoking with Self Hypnosis should be 22 min long
The Time Distortion should be 25 min long
Learning to Relax should be 40 min long
Sleep Better should be 15 min long
Smoking Cessation II should be 15 min long
Hypnosis Benefits should be 25 min long
Silky Breathing should be 25 min long
Staying Committed should be 25min long
Get Rid of The Compulsion should be 35 min long
Suggestions should be 35min long

"…" means take a breath while speaking before you continue.

PAUSE (for a few breaths)

LONGER PAUSE (give time to allow the listener time to imagine what you've suggested)

Introduction

Thank you for choosing **Quit Smoking Hypnosis audio**...And choosing this audio only means, you have taken a step towards loving yourself even more. In the past, you have smoked innumerable cigarettes and seen the consequences of smoking on your body. It may have given you temporary pleasure every time you smoked one, but eventually it kills by damaging your lungs, mouth, and throat. It may have caused you feel guilty of knowing

Quitting smoking is one of the best decisions you can make to live a healthier and happier life. And, it is never too late to quit. When you quit smoking, you increase your life expectancy, reduce the risk of lung cancer, high blood pressure, renal diseases, and sexual dysfunction. It also reduces the risk of respiratory complications.

The coughing will be reduced to quite an extent and you will have high levels of energy with better ability to taste food. The sense of smell and taste will improve significantly. Some of the other benefits of quitting smoking include better skin and improved complexion. The financial benefits are of course that you will save money.

This audio recording will not only reinforce the decision of quitting smoking but also reprogram your mind to relax your mind, body, and sleep better. This will help you manage your stress better and will eliminate the craving of picking up a cigarette significantly.

Pause

So, congratulations on taking this step of quitting smoking and making a wonderful decision to better health.

Pause

I would like you to sit or lay comfortably, where you will not be distracted. Do not listen to this audio when your mind requires your conscious attention.

Pause

Listen to this audio only when you are relaxed and stationary. Please use headphones so that you can focus on the sound of my voice.

Let us start...

Begin recording

Induction

You are now listening to the sound of my voice... and the sound of my voice only ...and as you continue to listen to each word I say...you allow yourself to relax more and more.

Pause

I wonder if you could take a deep breath...hold it for a count of 5... and then exhale.

Pause

Let's start now.

Breathe in Deeply...

Pause

Hold for a count of 5

1... 2...3...4...and 5

Now, exhale...
Pause

Once more, take another deep breath...

Breathe in...

Hold for a count of 5 — 1, 2, 3, 4, 5 (slowly)

Now, breathe out...
Pause

Once more, take another deep breath —

Breathe in

Hold for a count of 5 — 1, 2, 3, 4, 5 (slowly)

Now, breathe out

Pause

And, come back to your normal breathing pattern...

Pause

— And, I wonder… if you could simply bring all your focus and attention to the centre of your eye-brows…with your eyes closed…try to look at the centre of your brows and focus on the point between them…that's right.

Pause

In a moment, I am going to talk to that part of you, which is highly creative…the part that knows exactly how to help you imagine or create anything with the help of your mind's eye.

Pause

And… I know you can do it… because everybody can…we all have a creative mind, that has the ability and capability to create and imagine images in our mind.

I know you must have imagined or visualized or day-dreamed many times in your life. And… our creative part helps us imagine and visualize. Isn't it?

With the help of our creative mind, we can visualize, imagine, write, paint, and dream…and I am going to be talking to that part of you today.

Pause

Deepener

Imagine yourself standing on top of a 10 steps staircase and the staircase looks beautiful . As you look at it, you notice its handrails and steps. The staircase leads you to a hallway…and perhaps it is made of stone, wood, or metal, I don't know…but you know. Whatever material it is made of, just get the knowing of it. Feel the handrails with your hands.

You have the capability to imagine yourself standing on top of it…

And, as I count down from 10 down to 0…you notice yourself going down the staircase, starting with your right foot. And, as you go down, you will find yourself becoming twice as relaxed and twice as deep.

Keep your right foot on the top step…

10…let your body relax and feel or imagine yourself going into a beautiful state of relaxation
9…relaxing more and more, going deeper and deeper into the relaxing state of mind
8… getting comfortable and calmer
7…going deeper
6…even deeper and even more relaxed
5…half-way there
4…relaxing more and more with each step down
3…almost there and you can notice the door at the end of the hallway clearly
2…getting to the hallway in a moment…
1…deeply relaxed
0… you are at the bottom of the staircase.

Longer Pause

Be a Non-Smoker Script

And as you stand at the bottom of the staircase, you notice the walls and floor of the hallway and wonder what is behind the door.

You are going to move towards the door with every breath you take and with every word I say...

Pause

You are at the door and as you notice yourself at the door, you touch the door and feel its texture. Perhaps it's rough or smooth...and you notice its color and the door-knob or a handle.

You can listen to the sound of the birds and the wind blowing behind the door...

And, you know that there is a garden behind the door...and you can't wait to open it and explore it.

You are excited to push open the door and explore what lies behind.

Pause

So, slowly...you put your hand on the door knob or handle and push open it...and as you open it, you feel the fresh air on your face and smell the lovely fragrances coming from the flowers. The trees are tall and the grass is green...perhaps moist...

You look around and notice birds chirping and hopping from one branch to another and the trees sway with the wind. The wind caresses you gently as you look around and enjoy the beautiful surroundings.

In the center of the garden, you notice, a small cottage that looks beautiful from outside. The small staircase leading to its patio looks a bit worn out, but you are intrigued and want to look at it from inside.

Pause

The cottage attracts you and you excitingly open the door and reach the room that looks ashy and dark. It has a foul smell that you can barely stand and the walls look tarnished. The inside is completely opposite to the outside...the outside looks beautiful and polished while the inside looks quite raw and ugly...

You also notice the couch and the rug that look quite old. The upholstery of the ottomans and couches are all faded and have lost their sheen and glow.

Pause

It is almost impossible for you to stay indoors and you feel like going out in the beautiful garden to catch a fresh breath of air…
However, you feel a connect with this cottage and feel that it needs cleaning. For that, you magically get everything in the room to clean and refurbish it…because with the creative and powerful subconscious mind, you can create and imagine anything now.

Longer Pause

To make it look beautiful and clean from inside, you need to paint the walls, clean the floor, wash the rug, change the upholstery of the couches and ottoman…

And you have all the power to create a box of tools and everything you need to be able to do all this.

In a moment, you notice… a big box with paints, paint brushes, paint rollers, a ladder, vacuum cleaner, wipers, scrubbers, and many more tools to help you with painting and cleaning.

Pause

I give you a few moments to use your creativity to clean, clear, and make the room look absolutely new and beautiful.

Longer Pause (15 seconds pause)

Everything is neat and clean, the room smells fresh, the walls look beautiful, the floor looks clean…

The furniture has a new upholstery…perhaps its modern or traditional…but it's all new.
And, this makes you stay in here…and relax… as you continue to listen to me…

Pause

You believe that this is your cottage and you belong here…and to be able to stay here, the space needs to be clean and fresh…always.

Perhaps it now looks incredibly beautiful…organized and clean.

Pause

You know now that to be able to even stand in a place, it needs to be clean and fresh. It needs to look nice and should give you a feeling of warmth.

With all that you have changed in here, you not only can stand, but can stay and relax for as long as you want…

And this only means that you would want to keep it this way forever…clean and organized…smelling nice and fresh….no more shady, dark, dull, and smoky…

Deep Relaxation Script

As you continue to listen to me, you drift further and further into a beautiful state of relaxation. Continue to focus on the sound of my voice and the sound of my voice only.

Take a deep breath and let it out slowly.

That's right. Let's take another deep breath. Inhale ….and exhale.

And begin to let any tension from the body move away from you…as you continue to breathe normally and continue to listen to each word I say.

Continue to go further deep into this incredible state of relaxation. Imagine tightening your first very hard as if all the muscles are tensed up….and in a moment, simply loosen up and let go…

Pause

Let's do it with the other hand…tighten your fist and loosen it. Let both the hands go loose and limp. Let them go really relaxed and limp as if they cannot be relaxed any further.

And, now take all your attention to your eyelids, squeeze them hard and after a few seconds, simply let them be relaxed. Let go loose and relaxed…

I wonder if you can send a wave of relaxation to all your body parts starting from your head to the calves of your legs to the soles of your feet. Let your whole body go limp and loosen every part of your body...like a rag doll.

Pause

And the second wave of relaxation from top to bottom that makes you relaxed even more. Allow each muscle to be fully relaxed and you continue to listen to me and feel deeply relaxed.

Now allow your feet to completely become relaxed. And let your soles, ankles, and heels get beautifully relaxed.

Now, send the third wave, as they say that it's more like a charm. So, send the wave through the body from top to toe and see the muscles getting deeply relaxed.

Pause

And this relaxation begins to move up in to the calves of your legs, thighs, and hips. Let all the muscles in your lower body get completely relaxed. In reality, there is no stop to the amount of relaxation you can experience.

Now, let this beautiful feeling of relaxation move up in your torso, chest, and shoulders. Feel the relaxation moving into your upper back, middle back, and lower back…

It continues to move up again to the shoulders, neck, back of your neck, and to your face, relaxing every muscle, nerve, and fibre in your face.

You can easily feel the wave of relaxation in your face, your forehead, the top of your head…making every part in your eyes, eye lids, forehead go absolutely relaxed.

Pause

There is no limit to the relaxation you can experience. And, as I count down from 3 down to 1, with each count down, you will allow yourself to go even deeper with every count down.

Starting at 3…feeling the relaxation everywhere in your body…drifting down and down..

2…becoming even more relaxed…
1….even deeper…

As you continue to listen to the sound of my voice, you are being guided into the relaxation and the deeper you go, the more relaxed you feel, and more relaxed you feel, the deeper you go.

It is just a continuous cycle of deepening relaxation and feeling the feelings of comfort and relaxation. All you can experience right now is the calm and peaceful feelings all inside your body and all over it and as I count again down from 3 down to 1…you can double the relaxation.

Pause

Starting now at 3….double it up
2…going deeper and deeper
1…even more relaxed…

And as the mind relaxes, the mind gets further relaxed. And you can use this relaxation technique anytime you crave a cigarette.

Pause

Remember its all about diverting thoughts of smoking to doing something productive or better and with the help of that, you will be able to relax your mind and relax thoughts about cigarettes.

You would gain better control on your thinking and you will be able to change the action that follow the thoughts.

Inner Child Healing

As you continue to listen to me, you drift further down into this beautiful state of relaxation. You continue to listen to listen to me and that only reinforces the fact that you are serious about non-smoking and living a healthier and positive life.

In a moment, you are going to go back in your past to the first time you picked up a cigarette.

Pause

And, I know you can do it because everybody can. You are going to go back to the time when you picked it up and started to smoke. I am going to count down from 10 down 0 and with each count down, you are going to go deeper into your subconscious mind and reach that time when you first picked it up .

Starting now…at 10, 9, 8…..7……6…..5…..4……3…….2……….1….and 0.

Longer Pause (10 seconds)

You are at the time when you first picked up a cigarette. In your mind, look at the situation….did anyone tell you to try it or you just happened to do it on your own?

Just know the reason and go further back in time when you did not use to smoke at all. The time before the time when you picked it up. The time when you were happy, joyful, and had no stresses of life.

Even younger….that's right.

Longer Pause

Perhaps you are very young…and at school or home. Just look at what's happening around you…and the kinds of clothes you are wearing. Look what you are doing and saying. Notice your younger self closely.

Look at the expressions, the hair, and the skin.

This is your inner child and just imagine if you had a son or daughter like her, would you love her or him? I am sure you did…because as a parent, you would give unconditional love to this child, isn't it?

Pause

Today you are going to meet the child and have a conversation with them about how much you love them. How much you are ready to protect them and guide them in future.

You know that you are much wiser self since you have gone through all the situations that this child will go through. And, you will guide him or her about every future situation and allow them to move through them with all your support, love, and guidance.

You give them some pieces of advice and pearls of wisdom.

And, together you will travel in future when this younger self gets older and is about to pick up his or her first cigarette.

Longer Pause

You both are in the time in future when your past self is about to pick up a cigarette. And, because you have been through this situation and know all the ill effects of smoking. I would like you to speak to your past self about the bad effects of smoking and how it can affect the health.

Know that you have promised your younger self that you will always protect, guide, and take care of them.

So, what would you like to tell your past self as they are about to pick up a cigarette? I want you to have a conversation with him or her and let them know all the effects of it and what you experienced health wise when you smoked cigarettes. Talk to them about how difficult it was to quit and how many times you relapsed.

Longer Pause (10-15 seconds)

And, do not let this past self of yours pick up a cigarette. And, that only means that he or she will remain smoke free for the rest of their life.

The time has come to move forward together and come back to the present time. And, when you are together, you congratulate the past self to listening to you. You appreciate them.

You are a part of your past self and the past self is a part of you….you are both together right now and in a moment, the past self is going to integrate itself into you so that you become whole and complete. You will become one entity that does not smoke and stays healthy for the rest of your life.

Imagine, visualise, or notice, both of you becoming one with each other….imagine the past self is integrating into you and as that happens, you become even more confident, happier, joyful, and strong headed about not smoking. Together as one entity, you are going to live a happier life, a smoke free life, a fulfilling life.

That's right.

Increased Self Confidence

Continue to stay in the deep and focused state of mind, every breath you take allows you to maintain and deepen this miraculous state of mind. Your subconscious mind is infinite and powerful...which can take in all the positive statements and suggestions to help you achieve your goal of sticking to non-smoking and I know you can do that.

Pause

Your wonderful subconscious mind is open to every advantageous idea that I am saying which will bring positive changes to your emotional, mental, and physical well-being.

And with every heart-beat, it gets reinforced into your mind that you are listening to me because you have made a decision to quit smoking. And you continue to listen to me, till the time you are free from it.

Longer Pause

The sound of my voice further relaxes you deeply and helps you to reinforce and strengthen every positive idea said in this recording.

Just continue to float in this beautiful state of mind, let go, and feel calm. Simply enjoying this state, feeling absolutely calm and relaxed.

And, the conscious mind of yours wanders and let it do that...perhaps it goes far away or falls asleep and the inner mind of yours pays attention to me for the ideas that will make your health and life better.

Pause

And this subconscious mind brings out the memory from your childhood where you were absolutely confident, stress free, and secured. Your allow your subconscious to help you find that memory…

Longer Pause

And as you notice that memory from your childhood, you wonder that how can a person this confident and stress free pick up a habit of smoking? This is strange, isn't it?

Longer Pause

Perhaps the self-doubts, fears, or stress made you pick it up to lessen stress or to feel confident, and to think better to clear self-doubts. And, that's what cigarettes do with consequences of affecting your health for life.

Pause

And with this insight today, you are more than happy to let go of fears and self-doubt and living your life with self-confidence is the way to kick any habit that does not do any good to you. And kicking it will allow you to live a joyful and healthy life.

Know that self-doubt and fear are learnt feelings and you can simply unlearn them. What is learnt can be unlearnt because you were not born with it. Isn't it?

Your natural state is to be confident in every situation and with that confidence and assertiveness, you can say **No** to cigarettes.

Pause

The natural state of any person is exactly like a baby. Babies are born free, they laugh, cry, and do many things without any inhibitions. They are absolutely confident.

And you are that kind of a baby…just a grown up one now. And you learnt so many things as a child…learning to walk, ability to walk and get up again after falling, learning to speak, learning to run, you were incredible as a child and you are still.

This was your natural confidence and you would not have done that if you were not confident. Isn't it?

Pause

And no fear, self-doubt, and stress can stop you from achieving what you want to achieve. You are courageous, persistent, confident, and strong.

Your inner mind is full of all the knowledge that you need to know right now. It is the wisest part of you and that part gives you all the guidance about smoking cigarettes.

I am going to be quite for a few moments here so that you have a conversation with the wisest part of you.

Longer Pause (15 seconds pause)

After talking to the wisest part of you, I know you that you are feeling better and you know exactly what you need to do to feel healthy.

From today on, you will be a non-smoker who loves himself or herself fully, completely and deeply. You are someone who wants to enjoy life to the fullest and till the life exists for you. You can live longer without cigarettes and enjoy more gifts of life and gain more experiences.

Light the Fire Within – Empowering Yourself

You continue to relax yourself with every breath you take and go deeper and deeper into your own mind…turning all your awareness inside.

You are reaching the quieter and deeper parts of yourself..

Pause

And you do not have to worry about anyone and anything because the world is taking care of itself without you. All you have to know is that this is your time. The time to be with yourself , to explore yourself, and reach the deepest state of mind.

All your worries, tensions, stresses, thoughts are simply fading away as you focus on the sound of my voice.

You are open to receive all the powerful suggestions that I have to say. There is no need to remember anything, all you have to do is to just listen.

Just let this experience seep into every part of you…that's right.

Pause

And, here and now, you can make possible powerful changes, which are helpful to achieve all that you want to achieve. All that is going to be easy and effortless. When you have made the changes and you come out of this state and go back to the physical world, the changes made here will stay with you.

All these changes regarding your health will stay with you because you want them to stay with you and you want these to be permanent changes.

You can accept that only when you want the changes to stick with you, they stick with you.

Longer Pause

You trust yourself and believe in yourself that you can do it. You can make the changes and you allow them to be with you permanently.

And we will be working together on the changes and you let those changes go deep into your subconscious to make permanent impression in your mind, body, and soul.

As we progress into this, you are beginning to notice that that there will be a change in your behaviour and actions. And these changes will happen everyday for your highest good.

Your brain accepts these changes and you notice new neural pathways being created. And all actions and behaviours regarding the change will only strengthen these neural pathways.

You have the power to change what you want to change. The habit of smoking to habit of drinking water…and you can make all these necessary changes now.

Longer Pause

You can allow a deeper sense of comfort to reach every part of your body and mind. You are unaware of any distractions and you are only focused on each word I say.

You are now deeply relaxed and your mind is beautifully relaxed and open to every word I say to you. You accept these words because these words will allow you to make the necessary changes for you to have a healthy and fulfilling life.

These words have the immense power because you trust these words without any judgement..

Pause

That's right.

You will begin to relax even more and less reactive in situation and to other people. Every day you are becoming calmer and even more relaxed and have more mental clarity. You will stay composed and would be able to think twice before reacting to anyone or any situation.

You acknowledge that you want to remain calm and listening to every word I say only reinforces it. You mental, emotional, and physical wellbeing is enhancing and getting better with every passing day. You are now going to think clearly and focus better. You accept that there is nothing to worry and you are a person with infinite possibilities.

Pause

You do not let any remark from others affect your emotional and mental wellbeing. You love yourself a lot and you won't let it affect by anyone else's negative comments.

They are of no importance to you.

For too long now, you have held yourself back and perhaps the negative thoughts about yourself or the world around you have held you back.

Maybe you have felt too controlled in the past and perhaps that was because of the negative emotions. And, you rise above those negative emotions and feelings and cut the cords with the past now. Your past no longer affects you. And as you do that, you feel free, stronger, and lighter.

Pause

You no longer feel weighed down by all those past negative thoughts and feelings. . You feel much lighter and stronger. You are coming into the light, the beautiful light of peace and calm.

You rise above and feel lighter as if you are floating in the air, feeling absolutely relaxed and calm.

And as you notice yourself floating in the air, you notice fluffy clouds all around you. You can feel the softness, fluffiness, and lightness all around you and inside of you. This calm, soft and light feeling reaches every part of your body, in all the places of your being that need to feel calm and relaxed.

Longer Pause

The feeling of lightness is all around you and inside you and you can begin again to build deep sense of appreciation for yourself, strength, confidence, and high self- esteem. You are no longer weighed down by grief or pain. Everything seems so light and you feel free. That's right.

You let all the strength and confidence grow inside of you and you feel it all around you.

You truly accept that you are the person who deserves to be happy and confident. And, it is wonderful to appreciate the changes you have made and want to make for your own good.

Pause

You become aware of all the changes you know are possible and the changes you want to make, related to your health. These are the changes that are right for you. These changes help you accept yourself as happy and strong person.

Pause

You are fully in control and you have taken control of your life and body. With the changes you have made and are willing to make, you have a new sense of being renewed. As that happens, you notice yourself approaching a door that leads you to your future.

Longer Pause

The future that you are creating for yourself, the future that will show you as a changed person for your good.

And the colour of the door is purple and you push open the door, you enter the space of purple colour. All you notice around is purple - mesmerising colour. And you feel so calm and relaxed in this space. Also, feel focused and confident.

This is your future…

And close the door behind you with everything locked behind that does not solve any purpose. That does not do any good to you.

Longer Pause

You have amazing skills and talents that you have been honing for many years. And all this was possible because you believed in yourself. And from beginner to advanced, you changed. You changed your skillset, you got better. All this was possible because of your creative mind and spirit.

Pause

This an extraordinary space to be. You believe in yourself, you love yourself, you love your capabilities, you are confident. You believed that all the changes you made, worked. You have been changing knowingly or unknowingly ever since you came into this world. With the same belief, you can change any habit. You can change your mindset.

And, I know you can quit smoking and you have already done that by listening to me.

Quit Smoking Confidence

And let's imagine that you know all the negative effects of smoking and how it affects your breathing. You may have experienced how smoking has led you to breathe harder, perhaps it has been an effort to breathe.

It may have led to the irritation in the throat and caused you to cough perhaps while with someone at work, or in office meetings or at home…and so much of strain while coughing and the lungs getting grey and smoky air, may have caused quite some damage internally, which is perhaps not visible as yet on the outside.

And, I am sure you know of people who lost their lives to lungs or mouth cancer. Do you know what must have happened to their families?

Longer Pause

Imagine, what will happen to your family and how will you be missed?

Pause

And you are just imagining the future if you continue to smoke the cigarettes. But you can change all this and make it a beautiful future, where you are living a fulfilling and healthy life if you stop cigarettes now.

A beautiful family, work and social life.

You will be breathing clean and fresh air, healing your body fully from inside and looking amazing on the outside.

And all this is possible when you stop smoking NOW.

That's right.

You will live freely with clean and healthy body.

And, you have been a non-smoker already since you last smoked a cigarette. And, the body has started to heal already and you can continue doing that…and continue to heal your body.

Every time you think of a cigarette, you only think of all the bad it has done to your body and what it would continue to do if you choose to continue to smoke.

Pause

By knowing this, you feel a sense of confidence that you can control the urge to smoke and feel great about yourself and your body.

You feel in control. That's right.

And anytime you have an urge to smoke, you will intentionally look at the future in your mind where smoking has done damage to your health so that you know that its right to distract your mind and thoughts to something better.

You can divert your thoughts to drinking water or chewing a gum, or doing something else physically so that you distract your mind completely from smoking to non-smoking.

Pause

And as you divert your mind and thoughts to something else, you notice that with every passing day, your health becomes better and your body blossoms like a garden. And, you decide to take care of your body as your own house.

Pause

You ensure, everything is spick and span, you do not let anything bad come into your house, whether its pests, wild animals, rain water…that you know can damage your house or you. Similarly, you take care of your body just how you take care of your house. Keeping it absolutely neat and clean.

That's right.

Your mind says " No smoking" and you listen to it. You listen to it because your mind is very powerful. It knows what is right for you and what is not. And, the same mind is listening to me because it wants you to quit smoking. Isn't it?

I know you can do it, because everybody can.

Pause

Sometimes, your body may think that it's the boss and would let you pick up a cigarette because it craves it. However, know, that your mind is more powerful than your body and your mind wants you to not smoke and be a non-smoker for the rest of your life.

You want to be healthier, happier, and even more confident…living a happy and fulfilling life.

Longer Pause

You know every time you get a thought of smoking a cigarette, you will divert your mind to do something better and productive. You can choose to drink water, talk to your friends, do household work, or anything else.

That's right.

Stop Smoking Script

Your urge to smoke is not there anymore. HABIT CYCLES, the gorge of your primary complication - that's our concern at present.

Remember!! You are the creator of Habits and you can easily be the destroyer.
To do that, there is a way and that is to make you smoking conscious.

As soon as you get the urge to pick a cigarette, you will be aware of what you're doing.
And if you light it and start to smoke, you will be exceptionally conscious of every single time you indulged in smoking.

Pause

You have become oblivious to smoking, you have been doing it unconsciously. And that's the reason for your perpetuation.

But you are conscious now. The moment you go for that one cigarette, you will think with apprehension.

The moment you get acquainted with your actions, you are no longer a part of the vicious habit cycle.

And now it becomes easy. You know it. You don't want to smoke anymore. With your will power, the path becomes effortless and you know it. There will be no guilt.

Pause

Your consciousness will make you hate smoking. Perhaps you might even stub out the cigarette when you're halfway there. You will hate it.

You wouldn't want to carry on with it. You have got the reason why you smoke and you have made your mind up to put an end to smoking once and for all.

That's it. It's settled. You're done with it. Not tomorrow, not the day after, TODAY! At this very moment, you have already decided to end the habitual cycle. You are not going to smoke any more. No more.

You know the reason why you want to stop. Keep reminiscing about it. The reason is as clear as a crystal in your head.

Pause

Keep reminding yourself of the effects of smoking.

You are quitting because you want to. Without cigarettes there is no coughing, there is no pain, there is no trouble. Without cigarettes there is relaxation, there is rest, there's a feeling of security, happiness towards yourself and your loved ones. You're giving up troubles and gaining what you've always wanted.

Cigarettes is the thing of past

Buying a cigarette will be unnecessary as you don't smoke them anymore. As a result, you will desist to purchase them. Even if you accept a cigarette unknowingly, Straight away you'll be conscious towards it and a sudden impulse will try to restrict you to consume it. Next time, you'll break it into pieces whenever you get hold of it.

Pause

It will make you realize the bad effects it has on you and all the stack of goods that are waiting for you when you say No.

You will start to perceive the extent of marvellous good things you gain as compared to the bad ones you are leaving behind. As a result, restricting yourself from smoking will become a piece of cake.

Pause

Giving up things you do not like is easy and cigarettes is certainly one of them. Isn't it?

Feeling proud will be the side product of you being sober. It will become effortless to vanquish other habits. Altogether you will feel self-confident, self-assured, and self-reliant. You will be conquering your Life.

Every day you will feel evocative towards the grand step which made you happier. You'll start to count the days, weeks eventually the months along your journey. You'll come out as a speaker in your community to change others' lives as well.

Pause

You'll start to enjoy this journey. Keeping a record of the days of being an abstainer will become your diary to remember and to speak about. In time, keeping the record will not be necessary as you've conquered your habits and they no longer have the power over you. The rest of your life will be like a story to tell.

Habits are self-preserving. They are created in your mind. The power of your conscious mind is the only power that can dethrone them.

You are stronger than this habit. Now it's you versus the tobacco and you desire to come out as a winner. Patience, perseverance, calm, and relaxed determination are all your tools to fight this monster.

It's unshakable. One day at a time patiently. Counting each day as a success. Success will become habitual. And sooner, the love of success will become extensively grandiose than any habit has ever been.

Smoking Pros and Cons

You have been polluting your body for a very long time…perhaps your lungs are filled with toxins that are damaging your body and you have decided to give up smoking and that is why you are listening to this recording. You have taken the first step to loving yourself even more. And, that is amazing.

Pause

You will not put it off until tomorrow because that is what you have been trying to do for the past many years. Today is the day to quit smoking and be free from all the toxins to live a healthier and happier life.

Pause

Today, we are going to reinforce the desire to quit smoking, which is indeed good for your health and life. You will quit it once and for all. You know that smoking leads to cancer, which is painful and an expensive treatment. The very thought of smoking a cigarette reminds you of cancer.

The thoughts about going through the series of tests, chemotherapy, losing hair makes your desire to quit smoking stronger. You cannot let yourself go through that just because one cigarette gives you pleasure for 5 minutes.

Pause

You are smart and intelligent who has started to love health and body more. And, an intelligent person analyses and sees the pros and cons of situations and things. What according to you are the pros and cons of smoking a cigarette. Perhaps it relaxes you and makes you calm for 5 minutes, but it does long term inner damage, which can come to the surface anytime in the form of a disease.

Longer Pause

The cons are bad breath, smelly hair, hands and clothes, inability to fall asleep, coughing, breathing problems, damage of lungs, tar and nicotine stains on teeth, and spending too much on cigarettes.

Longer Pause

And, before I move ahead with what I have to say, I would like you to make a mental commitment to yourself, promise yourself that you will never pick up a cigarette. Looking at all the cons and ill effects smoking brings, I am sure, you are going to quit smoking.

I would love you to understand that your powerful subconscious mind accepts everything that I say for your highest good. It does not and will not question and will only accept what you and I are telling him. Your promise and commitment to yourself goes straight into your subconscious mind and the thought becomes stronger and stronger.

Longer Pause

You are now committed to the decision of quitting smoking more than you have ever been before. Your imagination is much more stronger and powerful that your will. And the creative part of you, will help you imagine that you have destroyed all the packs of cigarettes at home and at work.

Pause

You put a fire to them for good. With every passing minute, you are thankful that you have been able to commit yourself to the decision that will change your life and health.

Pause

You will have a better relationship with yourself. You will smell good, there will not be any tar and tobacco stains on your teeth. You will smell fresh and your breath will be fresh.

Your health will start to improve with every passing day. You will breathe fresh air, you will enjoy every moment of your life breathing fresh and with more mental clarity. You will not have any guilt that you perhaps used to have after smoking a cigarette.

You will be free and happy.

Longer Pause

And these suggestions grow stronger and stronger with every passing minute, hour, and day. You are a non-smoker - and you are proud to be a non-smoker.

Road to Stopping Smoking

Life is about the conscious choices you make, and you often find yourself at different crossroads of life. This particular time, you realize that the road you have taken so far as a smoker is too long, and it goes on for many more miles.

Pause

You find yourself at yet another crossroads yet again. This time, you are considering taking a different path, but you are confused about which road to take, the road less taken, or the one which will change your life. You are demented about what changes this road is going to bring.

Pause

Here's a thought, let's continue walking on the path you have always taken. Let's explore this familiar path and see what's in the store for your life if you continue to smoke.

Keep walking this way. While sauntering along this old path, you will see things that are associated with smoking.

You will see those gifted ashtrays that are now overflowing with cigarette butts, you will see that thick cloud of smoke that gets into your lungs leaving you to wheeze, and gasp for breath along the way.

Longer Pause

You are now more conscious about how your clothes smell. It opens your eyes, and you start to keep your distance from non-smokers because your self-respect is taking a hit. You feel embarrassed about how awful you smell when you are with your friends.

Now that you are seeing yourself from a third person's perspective, you are also seeing other people smoke. They are wheezing, coughing, and gasping for breath the like you did.

Pause

While walking, you come across this familiar hospital, and you suddenly remember someone you know is admitted there. They are gasping for breath and desperately reaching out for a nebulizer. There is nothing you can do to help this person, so you are only able to feel sympathy for them.

As you continue walking along this path you see your future. You see that you are with your children, grandchildren, and babies who you aren't allowed to hold in case you breathe on them and leave that stale unpleasant smell behind.

You are now short on money, but you are still trying to put it all together to buy a pack of cigarettes and smoking each one of them. It is a metaphor of how you are setting fire to not only your money but also your life. You are looking for each penny to buy poison and trying to kill yourself with that.

Longer Pause

When you see your hands, you are disgusted by them; they are stained because of the nicotine. They are now smelly, and your skin starts to feel nauseating and dirty. That irritating tickly cough just won't go away, so you are coughing and wheezing all the time.

Pause

You are now alienated from your group of friends, no one tries to approach you. In the office, you have to go outside to smoke and nobody accompanies you because of your toxic habit. Your co-workers start to step away from you, as you see them holding their nose trying not to inhale that stench.

How does it feel?

I am sure you are feeling bad about picking up this habit but you have decided to let go of it...isn't it?

Pause

You see your beautiful house ruined by the burn marks - the furniture has that unpleasant smell, and there are yellow stains on the wall because of the smoke, your heart breaks a little.

You walk towards the end of the road, and you see yourself lying on that hospital bed, like that friend you saw before. You are now scared for your life, as you see yourself fighting for the last breath. The things that you saw along your path are horrific, and they are now deeply carved in your mind forever.

Pause

Let's move on from the unpleasant imagination and feelings for now because none of them has happened to you yet, and it won't if you don't let it. You have reached that crossroads of life where you have to make a concrete decision of life or death. The fact that you are here today means a lot; that you want to correct your life; that you want to make these necessary changes to lead a happy life.

You have caught a glimpse of those vile things that could happen to you if you continued to walk on that road. I want to show you a glimpse of what life would be like if you take that new road to non-smoking.

Pause

The air is different on this road because it is clean and smoke-free. You get a crystal clear picture of everything, and you breathe in the pure air around you.

Notice how refreshing it is, it could last forever if you continue to walk on this new road. The fresh air fills your being with renewed energy and vitality. Even during this short span of non-smoking, you find that you're feeling better and healthier than ever before.

Longer Pause

Notice how your breathing has become easier than ever before. Your chest feels comfortable, and your throat is clearer. Your skin feels way better, and your fingers have no odour of cigarettes.

You start to smell good, as your clothes, skin, and hair are now clean. You now have that lovely, fresh, clean smell that is delicate, and you have that faint perfume by which people instantly recognize you.

Pause

If you observe keenly, you will realize that people are now idolizing you because you kept your word. People start hanging out with you again.

You are now a person of your words. Your conscious decision to quit smoking once and for all has brought people closer to you. The people you love are now close to you because you smell like integrity and trust.

On the new road, instead of a hospital, you see an entertainment centre where there is a sports complex or a gymnasium. Imagine some other place where you would enjoy keeping your body and mind healthy; where you will be yourself living your ambitions. Go to those places with your near and dear ones or with your peers that you have inspired by making a healthy choice to become, and remain a non-smoker for the rest of your life.

Pause

Your confidence level is so high that you rely on yourself instead of props or addictions. You become a confident and self-assured person. You have this wonderful feeling of achievement and attainment of wellbeing, after quitting smoking.

Your home has now become the most beautiful place on this earth for you. It is just so beautiful, and peaceful that you enjoy staying there.

You love this new you. You love it that you are a non-smoker now because it feels wonderful. It just increases your determination to be that way forever.

Keep the Motivation Going

Once you have lived that amazing non-smoker life, you are now motivated to live that life every day. Every day you feel better, healthier and the best version of yourself you have ever been. You radiate more energy, vitality, and you feel really good about yourself.

As you walk along the road of being a successful non-smoker, I wonder if you can see, sense, or feel yourself, after it's quite a long way past that crossroad of your life.

Imagine the future you, you have been a successful non-smoker, and you are feeling proud of yourself for being consistent.

Pause

The road is lovely, as it is full of flowers and greenery growing on both sides. You notice that being a non-smoker is paying off well, as endless opportunities are arising for you, and your confidence increasing because you feel so much better about yourself.

Do you realize how much money you have saved by not smoking? You could so much with that type of money. The small incremental savings daily will come back to you in heaps. You could purchase something special for yourself, perhaps a new outfit or something to compliment your home.

Pause

You could put in a deposit for a holiday, it doesn't matter what you do with the money, so long as it's something special for you. You deserve something amazing because you are special, you deserve to treat yourself, and you deserve to feel proud of yourself.

Longer Pause

You have become this wonderful human being who sticks by his/her words. You proved that you are consistent and you meant what you said when you stopped smoking completely.

You have come so far in life that I wonder if you could rewind for a second and go back to the time where you used to smoke.

Now, imagine that one of your toxic friends is there, a friend who smokes a lot and is offering you a fag.

Pause

You see them taking out a case of cigarettes. They are slowly but carefully unwrapping the cellophane from it. They are further opening the case and pulling the cigarettes out halfway to offer you one.

While this whole scene is taking place, you realize that the person is not your true friend. A true friend will never tempt you when you are so determined to remain a non-smoker.

Pause

Do you hear yourself say 'No' to cigarettes and meant it? Do you realize that your mind and body are rejecting cigarettes? Now that you know that cigarettes are like a poison to your system, you don't want them, you don't need them, so as a result, you don't have them.

Longer Pause

When you say 'No' to cigarettes, an amazing thing happens, you experience a wonderful feeling flowing into your being. It fills your very existence with pride, confidence, and a sense of achievement.

You feel fresh, so you say 'No' to cigarettes, and you mean it. You decline the offer because you're a non-smoker now, and that's the way you prefer to be.

Every day you feel better and healthier and happier, you have more confidence and more vitality and you feel good because you are a non-smoker now. You are a non-smoker and that's the way you do prefer to be.

Pause

This feeling only gets stronger. You become more determined and motivated which makes you feel better, happier, healthier, and fitter than ever before.

Now that you are a non-smoker, you prefer to be one forever. These suggestion grow stronger every day, as they become more profound, powerful, and more important to you.

Smoking Cessation

Imagine that you are entering a special room. Now, when you look around, you see that your room is filled with beautiful lights and wonderful colors. Do you notice how your room is furnished and the air is clean around you?

Now, imagine that the air you are breathing is filled with thousands of tiny molecules of clean and pure energy. Every molecule penetrates deeply into your chest and flows right into your lungs because the air quality is pure.

Pause

Now, you see yourself from another perspective, as a non-smoker. Did you notice how much better you look now that you've stopped smoking? Your complexion is clearer, your breath is fresh, and your mouth tastes cleaner. You have more energy and vitality, your eyes are sparkling, and so you look, and feel better than you've ever felt before.

You feel relaxed, self-assured, and very confident about yourself. All your senses are sharpened, your food tastes better, your sense of smell is heightened, your mind is clearer, even your circulation is improved by giving up smoking.

Longer Pause

From this moment you are a non-smoker. You don't ever want to smoke because you don't like it and therefore you have quit smoking. Smoking was your thing in the past; it's something you used to do. You are a non-smoker now, and you are proud to be a NON-SMOKER.

When you are with other people who smoke you become extremely consciously of the stale and unpleasant smell of tobacco coming from them. You can smell that stale tobacco on their clothes, hair, breath, and even on the skin of every smoker that you come across.

Pause

You're disgusted by that stale smell of tobacco, it makes you feel nauseous, and the thought that you've been inhaling that poison into your body makes you feel sick, and that is exactly why you prefer NOT to think about cigarettes at all. It is also the reason that you made a firm commitment to yourself, to never smoke again. From this moment forward you have no desire, no need, no want, to ever smoke again.

Pause

You have created your world where there is nothing called smoking, at least not for you. Smoking was part of the old you, the dependent you, but this new you have more confidence. You are now in more control of how you feel, you feel happier and calmer than ever before.

Giving up smoking **makes** you feel more confident, it is a sign that you are in control of your mind, body, and your health. You enjoy this feeling of being in control. You love how that toxic part of you has vanished into thin air, you are now an ex-smoker, and you are PROUD to be an ex-smoker. You are proud of the fact that you could overcome something that you were struggling with for so long.

Pause

I suggest you to project your mind into the future, and imagine those six beautiful smoke-free months that have gone by where you neither had, nor wanted a cigarette.

These past six relaxing smoke-free months, you enjoyed being a non-smoker. You're feeling healthier, happier, cleaner, and more in control of your mind, body, and health.

Longer Pause

Imagine that you are allowing someone to come into this scene and that they are offering you a cigarette. They are offering the cigarette to you and your immediate reflex is a firm 'No'. You say 'No' to the cigarettes because your mind and body reject them. You don't want them or you don't feel the need to have them, so your mind decided not to have them.

When you say 'No', you mean it. You know that cigarettes are poisonous to your system, your mind. Your body rejects them as soon as the thought comes of a cigarette.

Pause

Saying 'No' to cigarette feels good because you love being in control of your mind. Now that you are in complete control of your body, mind, and your health, you are easily controlling your urges. You love being a non-smoker because it makes you feel good. It gives you confidence and control of your body.

Pause

Over the next few days and weeks you're going to be drinking lots of water because it will help you flush the nicotine out of your system, once and for all.

You love the taste of water and you know it help in flushing out the toxins and gives your face a beautiful glow. With every passing day, your mind becomes even stronger and you become even more in control of your health and urges.

Pause

You drink at least 8 to 9 glasses of water everyday

You are now a non-smoker and enjoy this amazing feeling of being free from the toxic substance. It's so refreshing to completely eliminate tobacco from your system. In no time, you will start to see the positive results in your breathing, throat, sense of taste and smell, and skin.

Appreciate Yourself

It would be great if you were appreciated by everyone all the time. It would be so good to be liked by all. Imagine never getting criticized or being treated unfairly by a single individual.

But what's not great is how you feel down all the time to anybody around you. It is not such a great feeling when your happiness seems to be out of your grip. Your happiness is your own responsibility and you can be the one who has control over it.

Pause

You are not seeking perfection, but only the sense of being a healthy human. You understand that perfection or perfectionism is unattainable.

And those who blindly run after it are only going to end up in disappointment. The craving for perfection is only going to consign one to a life of failure and frustration.

Your understanding of this is as why you will always have your humanity as your strength.

Longer Pause

You need to try to understand that there are people out there who like you for the way you are; with all your humanity and all your strengths. They see you as a fantastic person who is great, today, just being yourself. What can you possibly do about the few who don't appreciate you?

It will not matter to them even if you change your hair, your habits, your size, shape, clothes or your behaviour. Some people appreciate you today with everything that you have. Some believe that you need no change and cannot be better than this. Some might start appreciating you tomorrow or a week later.

Pause

The only thing that should matter to you is that you are honest to yourself. You should be the one who appreciates all your strengths and cherish and nurture them. Learn what you're good at and rejoice in it. You also need to understand and be just as honest about your flaws.

Pause

Try and work hard towards fixing anything that can be remedied. And as to any flaw you find no solution to, remember that there is no use by being overwhelmed or paralyzed by it. Make peace with yourself and your nature. Always work in the direction of progress to fix any flaws you feel, even if it's not speedy. The will to change is what will lead to change.

Longer Pause

Some people will think of you as a wonderful person while some won't. These opinions won't matter to you when you have embraced yourself. When you know all your strengths and work on changing the inescapable for yourself, you are at ease with the judgments of others. You work on yourself with a cool head and a calm heart.

Pause

No matter where you are, with friends or family, you welcome both praise and criticism. It is great when somebody sees your strengths and agrees with you. It is also fine for people to disagree and not appreciate you. It is only human to make mistakes.

You know yourself with your humanity and strength. You accept you need to work on yourself quietly. The opinions of others hold no surprise for you anymore. People either agree and accept you or let them be wrong.

Pause

This day onwards, you only wish to eat food that is healthy and right for you. You eat the right quantities, at the right time for the right reasons. You are completely content and satisfied with your choice. You are getting slimmer, fitter, healthier and happier by the day. Not to forget, even more gorgeous.

Today, tomorrow, every day you feel good about yourself even from within. You are forever at ease with yourself. You like yourself and feel happy, settled, secure and satisfied naturally. You are more confident, optimistic, cool, calm and comfortable being yourself.

Sleep Better

And as you continue to listen to me, your imagination further expands and you imagine a brightly lit room. The room has a window through which you can you see the sunshine coming. Because the room is lit, you can easily see the walls and ceiling of the room with your thoughts everywhere. You can notice what thoughts keep you up and what thoughts keep you from falling asleep.

Longer Pause

For good health, it's important to sleep better and when you sleep well at night, you wake up feeling happy and fresh. Your brain functions better. So, to be able to sleep well at night, you need to clear all the thoughts from the walls, so that the room looks clean and as the Sun goes down, you start to feel relaxed and calmer.

Look around and carefully notice what all is written on the walls. Do they even serve any purpose?

Pause

Perhaps they are the thoughts from the past or future that stops you from falling asleep in the present.

There is no point in having these thoughts. Isn't it?

Longer Pause

The room looks chaotic because there is so much on the walls, floor, and the ceiling. What is the point in having such a room?

So, you decide to paint the walls new. Before that, you are going to scrape off all the thoughts with a sandpaper. You magically see the sand paper appearing in front of you. You take it in your hands and start scraping the walls, floor, and ceiling now.

Longer Pause

And once you have scraped off the thoughts from the floor, ceiling, and walls, you feel tired and relaxed.

So, you relax for a moment in the room and as you relax, you notice that the Sun starts to go down...and you start to feel even more relaxed.

The room has started to get a bit dark because the Sun light is moving away and in a moment, you will notice a big paint bucket with paint brushes and rollers appearing magically in the room.

Pause

And, with the powerful imagination, your start to paint the walls black so that it gets dark in the room and you start to feel even more sleepier and drowsier.

Start painting the walls black. Take the paint brush and start painting the walls and ceiling now.

Pause

That's right. Now start painting the ceiling black…

Longer Pause

Now, imagine putting a black rug on the floor, which is fuzzy and soft to touch. And as you feel the rug beneath your feet.

Longer Pause

And as you do that…you feel some weight has been lifted off your body and you instantly feel relaxed and calm.

Pause

There are no thoughts on the floor or ceiling or floor and all you can notice is the darkness all around you because of no Sunshine outside of the room, black painted walls and ceiling and black rug.

Longer Pause

The room now looks absolutely black from all sides…

It's comfy and you are not distracted…

You now allow yourself to count back from 5 down to 0…and with each count down…you will be twice as relaxed and twice as deep.

5…feeling relaxed
4…going deeper and deeper
3…relaxing more and more..
2…entering a deep state of relaxation
1…calmer and deeper

Affirmations for Sleep

I would now like you to repeat the suggestions after me..

It's so much more easier to let go of every thought about past and future every night (4-5 seconds pause)

I close my eyes and paint the room black in my mind when I want to sleep (4-5 seconds pause)

With every brush stroke, it's easier for me to let go and drift into a peaceful sleep (4-5 seconds pause)

I feel drowsier when I imagine yourself painting the room black (4-5 seconds pause)

My mind is relaxed and my thoughts slow down as soon as I hit the bed (4-5 seconds pause)

Stop smoking II

Congratulations! I'm very proud of you that you have made this important decision in your life. By listening to me, you have decided to become a non-smoker. If you pay close attention, you will realize that you always wanted to quit smoking, and that is what makes this very special, as you have finally decided to honour your body and quit smoking.

Pause

Your body barely liked you for treating it so badly; your toxic habits were hurting your body and you without your knowledge. It is beautiful that you are now finally doing something good for yourself. Nicotine is not the addictive part because if it was then people would have been addicted to alternatives like the nicotine patch or the nicotine gum. If it was addictive, then someone I would be doing this hypnosis therapy to make people quit the gum or the patch. Till now, it has never happened and I can ensure that it never will.

I wonder why people keep smoking, is it because it's a habit? But then again, what is a habit? It's when you automatically think about doing something and simply responding to a thought. Well, if that's the case then you don't have to do that anymore because you are free from smoking.

Pause

You subconsciously know that smoking is just your way of responding to a destructive thought. You should know that your thoughts have no power over you because when you look back you will realize that you have thought about doing thousands of things and then simply decided not to do them.

Pause

Remember the time when you decide to buy something but then changed your decision not to buy it because you thought that the money would be better spent on something else? It is the same thing with cigarettes. If you think about it, when it comes to spending your money, it is always better spent on something else than cigarettes.

Pause

Always remember that there is something better to do than smoke. It is not the nicotine in the cigarettes that are addictive, but it's the poison that is. There is only a small amount of poison in each cigarette, but even that tends to build up until your body becomes affected by it and you become sick. Sometimes it becomes a major illness like cancer, heart disease, or emphysema, and other times, it is something like a cough or bronchitis. You know the consequences so you have decided not to let any of those things happen to you. You are now strong and you have made a very strong decision to not let that happen to you.

Pause

You are very stubborn about sticking to being a non-smoker and to let go of all the worries and sickness associated with cigarettes. As you are grasping that fact, you are becoming free, so all of your urges start to fade away.

You have taken complete control, you are not going to allow yourself to be weak that will eventually make you sick, a mere thought. Have you thought about how this thought came into your mind? It's not like you were walking down the street one day and this idea popped into your head out of nowhere.

Pause

You must have got this idea from somewhere or it is also possible that you would have seen someone else smoking, and that idea clung on to your mind. You saw some else do it and somehow you thought it would be a good idea if you did it too, but have you wondered where did they get this idea from? If you think about it, everyone smokes for one reason - someone must have made some compelling points and sold it to them!

Today, you smoke because it is one of the most successful marketing plans in the history of the world. It started years ago when America entered WWII, and everyone was so sold on the idea of cigarettes that even the government was buying them to give it to our brave men and women who were fighting a war. As a result, most of those people came back with the smoking habit.

Longer Pause

We get influenced by the people we admire the most and that why we look up to our parents, role models, celebrities, and try to replicate their actions. Smoking is one of those traits that you pick up from these people and just because they smoke, you smoke too. This habit is just handed down to you and you take it because you want to look cool in front of your peers.

If you go down your memory to our previous conversation about WWII, you will realize that comparatively, people who die of smoking are more than the people who died in the great wars. These corporate companies are easily advertising this product for you to break down and once you fall for it, it's all over for you. Once you realize that it's all a setup, you are on to them and their advertising campaign no longer affects you.

Now you regret, you regret being sold that pack of lies in the form of your "stress buster". You now know that each pack of cigarettes is a pack of lies and smoking is now simply something you "used to do". You are free from the chain of a toxic decision you made a long time ago.

It will feel so good to be free, free from all the pain, and the worry. Every time you find yourself slipping, you will remember that there is always something better to do than to smoke a pack of lies. Now that you have quit smoking for good, you will have time to experience so many fun and interesting things to do.

Pause

The information that I'm giving you now is stored in your conscious and subconscious mind, so you no longer can accept poisoning yourself for any reason. You turn away from any form of tobacco, so you are free. Free from the urge and that poisonous chain.

You feel free, you feel so free and relaxed that you don't feel the need to smoke while going back after work. This day is your special day; you can consider it as important as your birthday or anniversary. When you look back, you will feel content because this is the day when you finally took back the control over your body.

Longer Pause

That implies, now you are in complete control of your body, you have finally got what you were longing for, for so long. Now that you are in control, you regret the fact that some poisonous substances controlled you for long and you didn't even know it. But instead of dwelling on your past mistakes, you should be celebrating the fact that no matter what happens; you will never lose control over your body again. You should feel because now you have all the time in the world and you can always do something better with it rather than poisoning yourself with cigarettes.

Remember that smoking is no longer connected to your life in any way, and all of those old self-harming connections are broken up with, completely. All those activities you used to do while smoking will now be even better because you are healthier now and there will not be any embarrassment, worry, or frustration of cigarettes! Now if you watch TV, visit a friend, or simply chinwag on the telephone, you are not worried about cigarettes.

They were dirty (filthy) and they made you sick, but now everything goes better with the health and confidence you find as a non-smoker. You are free from all the frustration and now smoking is simply something that you "used to do". You are now free because there is always something better to do than smoke.

There is always a gut feeling that your subconscious mind warns you about and you had that feeling about quitting smoking.

You always know that you would quit smoking one day and it worked so congratulations! This is not a feeling that you have just for a day and then you go back to square one, you have accomplished something that you will cherish for the rest of your life.

Longer Pause

You are free from smoking for today and the rest of your life. When you decided to quit smoking you took the initiative to quit all of your reasons as well. You made a great package deal. You made a great trade! You traded something toxic for something priceless and healthy.

If you think about it, no amount of money can add a day or two to your life; it completely depends on the quality of life you aspire to lead.

Pause

Do you realize how many people wish that they could trade something for more time, a longer life? You have traded smoking for something precious, a longer life. You are now going to live a higher quality of life. This new life of yours is going to be filled with time, money, and self-respect. It is going to give you more vitality and confidence to take on the world.

By now you should realize that if you don't have your health, you don't have anything. You have made a jackpot deal where you are trading something you don't want at all for something that will end up giving you happiness and health. Besides, now you have plenty of time to enjoy every minute of it. Remember your mantra as you make these new changes, smoking is simply something that you "used to do".

Longer Pause

If you broaden your perspective a little bit, you will realize that there is always something better to do than smoking your lungs out. Think about your past trauma, think about all the things you went through, you would never go back to the old ways since they are simply toxic. Smoking is never a good idea, it causes pain and you simply traded it for something better, good health. No matter how much withdrawal tests you, never go back to smoking, and always remember that you can handle your life without cigarettes.

Longer Pause

You are too good for smoking; you are so stubborn that you will reject a fag at any given circumstance. Always remember that there is something better to do than smoking and keep saying it to you like it is a mantra. The withdrawal from smoking will keep you free and in control forever.

Pause

Think about it, every time you want to smoke, drink water because having a drink of water is better, even chewing a piece of gum is better than smoking. Doing anything other than smoking (as long as it is not illegal, immoral, or fattening) is better than smoking.

You are in control; you handle these situations effectively like a boss. You are now in complete control of your body, so you will no longer poison it with that toxic habit. You are simply going to turn your back on all of that poison and as a result, your body will reward you with health. Your mind will reward you by thinking more clearly since the smoke has cleared.

Pause

Emotionally, you will feel better because you are free from all the worrying and stress of smoking. Smoking is simply something that you used to do. You traded it away for something priceless - life, health, self-confidence, and peace of mind. Congratulate yourself now because you are a non-smoker and you are going to be that way for the rest of your life. You are now least bothered by people who smoke around you and when they do, it only makes you proud of yourself. You feel proud of the fact that you are now in complete control of your body (even though you might feel a little sorry for them).

Longer Pause

When you are around smokers, the smoke and fire will not affect you in any way because you can enjoy the company of others that smoke, but not want it at all for yourself. You will always feel a little better (inside and out) knowing that you are back in control. You can be proud of yourself because cigarettes cannot push you around anymore. You are proud to be a non-smoker and you are going to be a non-smoker for the rest of your long healthy life.

Repeat this silently to yourself as I say it out loud, "I am now a non-smoker, and I'm going to be a non-smoker for the rest of my life." (Compound it 15 times).

Longer Pause

From this moment on, you are a non-smoker. You feel better than ever before and you are going to feel better yet, as your lungs continue to become healthier because you have gotten rid of all the tobacco poison.

Pause

You are thoroughly done with all the toxicity and the smell as there is a part of you that always hated it. You have always hated it because it is filthy, dirty, and it makes you sick to your stomach. You refuse to debate your decision because your mind is now made up. You are stubborn about quitting because when you think about cigarettes, you know that you will make that mistake never again.

Longer Pause

Now, if for any reason in your life, you think that you might want a cigarette, all you have to do is take a deep breath and as you exhale, just say to yourself, "There is always something better to do than smoke". Let yourself have that feeling of being in control. Let's try that exercise right now, take a deep breath, and as you exhale, say to yourself, "There is always something better to do than smoke." Notice how good it feels to be free from that old toxic habit. Add patterns that you can use if you have time. You are here today because you have made up your mind completely to become a non-smoker. You want to quit because you can no longer let cigarettes control your life.

You are now motivated. You are motivated to let go of the pain and suffering that comes with smoking. You are willing to face the world without smoking. You are hit by the fact that smoking is a real poison and a threat to your happiness. We will now try breaking all of the links that you have made between smoking and other things. Remember?

There is always something better to do than smoking, when you are bored, stressed, etc. Your desire for cigarettes is fading away to nothing and all the connections are completely dissolved. These new changes that you have been implementing into your life have changed you into a new person, a non-smoker. Your reactions to cigarettes as a non-smoker are opposite; you are irritated and a little revolted even by the smell of it. Non-smokers handle their feelings and emotions without cigarettes and react differently.

Pause

It is one of the many benefits that come with quitting cigarettes, you are not worrying about them, you are wearing fresh-smelling clothes, your breath, and health is way better. "I'm now a non-smoker and I'm going to be a non-smoker for the rest of my life!" When you are around others that smoke it will make you feel good to know that you are in control of your life.

Pause

If you ever have even the slightest thought of having a cigarette, all you have to do is take a deep breath, hold it, and slowly exhale and you will be back in control, feeling good about your new life.

White Light Meditation

With your eyes closed, picture a white light emerging through you forehead; reaching and relaxing every nerve, fiber, muscle in your body. When you think about your forehead, it smoothens and relaxes.

The light goes on to relax your eyes, face muscles and jaw. The place where all your tension and stress gather is your jaw. It is fine for you to open your mouth a bit to relax it. The white light reaches your neck and then your chest, relaxing them on its way. Every breath relaxes you more and more. It is the sound of my voice that relaxes you. You are letting go of any other sound that is unimportant to you.

Pause

The white light moves further down to your arms and hands. Every muscle relaxes slowly. It is perfectly fine for you to feel you palm warming up and a tingling sensation in your fingertips. You are finding it difficult to lift your arms as they feel heavier but much relaxed. As you now take a deep breath, your leg muscles loosen up all the way down to your toes. Your entire body has now lightened and become relaxed.

Longer Pause

You are now going to visualize a peaceful, special place for yourself. It is perfectly fine for you to choose anything for yourself, be it a beach or a mountain. You now notice a 10 step staircase that takes you down to this place.

Every step getting closer to this place doubles your relaxation. Standing on the 10th step, you drift deeper and deeper – step 9,8,7 and so on. As you slowly get of step one, you have finally arrived in you special place. In this special place, you are isolated from any disturbances.

Your mind is peaceful. You can come to this place anytime and let go of you daily life stress and tension. In this special place, you are always going to have a sense of peace and calm, well-being and any sign of stress will completely bounce off of you.

Pause

You are taking this journey of change with my voice, becoming more and more peaceful with every breath. The sound of my voice relaxes you.

You are now focusing on your eyes. Your eyes have reached to a stage of relaxation where they feel only like a piece of skin. In a few moments I will ask you to open your eyes on my count, but it will be in vain. You will notice that your eyes seem to be stuck together, unable to open no matter how much you try. Now, 1,2,3 – I am asking you to try and open your eyes. Try a little harder. Now, I want you to shift your focus and go in deeper into hypnosis.

Your mind is now open to my voice which has an ever increasing effect over your way of thinking and feeling.

Today is the first day of your non-smoking life. You have now become a non-smoker. This decision is fuelled by all the right reasons and a motivation to rid your body of this habit. You realize that giving up this habit makes space for you to take part in healthy habits such as drinking lots of water.

Pause

Your decisions let you lose an enemy and gain health. You will be successful in this endeavor just as you have been in your past ones. You are now the person you always wanted to be – a non-smoker. From now onwards, the thought of smoking cigarettes will repulse you.

Longer Pause

You understand that it is a disgusting habit that impeded your breathing. It also took away your ability to relax, creating boredom and reducing your self-esteem. But you have now had enough of this sickening habit that fills your system with dirt.

The smell of cigarettes has now become positively revolting for you. Imagine throwing away a pack of cigarettes. You need to be rid of this poison. So today, you are going to go home and clean out nay traces of your smoking habits.

Pause

You will find it refreshing to have every cigarette thrown out and clothes washed out to clean the smell. You can do all this because you are now a NON-SMOKER.
We are now going to place a new picture in your head. In this picture, you are standing in a spring flower meadow surrounded by Hyacinths, primroses, bluebells and daffodils - all the flowers that you love.

Longer Pause

You can also see English castle surrounded by water and a moat at some distance. Your curiosity asks you to explore it. You walk to the castle, open a creaking door and find yourself standing in the dark. Only a stream of light enters the castle through a turret. In this band of light, you see dirt.

Pause

You decide to pick up the spicket and scrubbing brush lying there and clean it all. You watch all the dirt go down the drain as you scrub and wash the walls. It takes a lot of water but you finally clean it and go back out into the meadows. As you step out, you are amazed by the awakening of your senses.

You can feel the fresh air blowing over your skin. You can sell the sweet smell of all the flowers. You now feel proud of yourself for putting in the work to clean up and you now lay down to rest and take a nap.

Tomorrow, when you wake up you will start your first full day of being a non-smoker. You feel great that you made the decision with all the right reasons and are carrying it through.

Pause

With every breath you take in, you trust your ability to set goals and achieve the. You are now a non-smoker. Try and visualize your life an year from now. You have finally made it.

It came very easily to you once you made a motivated decision. You realize that you have saved money for yourself in this last year and you give yourself a treat that day. This is all because you have put yourself in the centre of your universe. You are the best.

Longer Pause

You can now visualize the healing white light passing through every nerve and muscle and healing everything. You are now getting cleansed. Imagine that white light now passing on from you to those close to you – healing and cleaning them all. You are all the light.

Pause

You now have to remember this feeling of being a non-smoker and the white light. You want to be the light. You wish to be healthy. You are now a non-smoker who is healing his/her body with every breath he/she takes.

So now onwards, when you put your head on your pillow to sleep, remember that you will have the best sleep through the night and wake up fresh. You are going to be relaxed and fantastic. The first thing that you will say to yourself is – I am a non-smoker.

Sleep Reprogramming

As you continue to listen to me, you know that in your mind, there is a beautiful place, a place like beach, where your subconscious mind can program itself. The programming of mind will help you return to the ability you were born with. You an naturally fall asleep and stay asleep throughout the night, each and every night.

Your powerful subconscious mind can be much faster than what I say and has the ability to interpret and absorb the information. It keeps the information for a long time. And as I speak, your conscious mind can drift away to the beach. The beautiful beach with grainy brown sand and blue waters. The waves crashing against the seashore. And as you conscious mind drifts there, your subconscious accepts all that I am saying.

And your vast subconscious mind goes far ahead of me to act on every healthy things for you to sleep peacefully and better, every night. The more you listen to me, the more strongly every breath restores you to a peaceful sleep every night.

You let your subconscious mind know that how much you appreciate deep sleep as it allows you to function fully the next day, at home or at work. You tell your subconscious mind now that how important restful sleep is to you.

Longer Pause

You also tell your subconscious mind the bad effects of not sleeping on time and fully. It leads to crankiness, snapping at people, irritability, lack of focus and attention, low energy, and mental confusion.

Pause

And, allow your subconscious mind to understand the consequences of not sleeping well.

Longer Pause

Let your subconscious mind know what is it that you want it to do so that every morning you are awaken feeling fresh.

Tell your mind that you want to awaken each day feeling rested and refreshed. That, you want a restful, peaceful, and deep sleep every night.

You wish to be awaken every day feeling absolutely wonderful, positive, and motivated. You want to feel happy, energetic, and fully recharged. For this, of course, you want to be able to fall asleep faster and get up feeling recharged and refreshed.

Now, allow your subconscious mind to know all the benefits of sleeping on time and deeply.

Longer Pause

Your subconscious mind knows and accepts your new goal to sleep better and if there is an old pattern of sleeping less, that will simply fade away.

The part of your powerful creative subconscious mind monitors every word I say and locks in every positive idea for you. And, it has the ability to go deeper into your mind and reprograms everything for your highest good.

And, because you want to be able to get up feeling absolutely refreshed and recharged, you practice taking 3 deep breaths. Each breath will relax you and ground you. As you settle into your bed, you close your eyes and take three deep breaths. While you breathe in and breathe out, you practice imagining the color of positivity inhaling and the color of negativity exhaling.

That's right.

And, then imagining painting the walls and ceiling of the room completely black. This way you will start to feel drowsier and sleepier. And all through the sleep hours, you sleep peacefully and deeply.

Every muscle in your body relaxes and you can feel the fuzzy and soft black rug beneath your feet, giving you a beautiful and relaxed feeling.

Pause

And as you do so, you also say the word "Sleep Now" that your subconscious mind will know and recognize and because of all the reprograming, it will make you fall asleep.

Sleep Now is your magic word from now on and as you relax in your bed and preparing to fall asleep, you say the word as many times as possible, till you feel the need to fall asleep.

Pause

Everytime you repeat the word – Sleep Now to yourself, you automatically drift into a natural and peaceful sleep. And with every time you say it, you become more and more relaxed and calmer.

You enjoy restful and deep sleep. The next morning, you wake up feeling refreshed and relaxed.

Pause

You will be woken up by your Subconscious mind if at night there is any emergency or you feel the need to use the restroom.

And, you can go back to sleep by repeating the word – Sleep Now.

Everyone is born with a natural ability to sleep and that is why babies sleep and new borns sleep for upto 20 hours in a day. Sleep is not something to be learnt. It is natural and it will come to you when you allow it to.

Pause

And as you get into the bed, you imagine a beautiful blanket that is fuzzy, warm, and colorful covering you from all sides. This makes you feel comforted and safe at night. The colorful blanket has all the colors like orange, red, yellow, green, blue, violet, and white.

Imagine all the colors on you and around you NOW.

Pause

These colors swirls together all around you, over you, through you, keeping you warm and safe.

And as you look at each color in the swirl, you notice drifting further down in a beautiful state of relaxation.

In you mind again, repeat the magic word – Sleep Now.

Your mind has been totally re-programed for refreshing and full night's sleep. When you sleep better, you are less stressed and more relaxed and can easily handle day to day issues with your wise mind.

For that you do not have to pick up a cigarette. You only have to have a glass of water, imagine taking deep breaths, and believe in yourself…that you can do it.

You are a non-smoker

You love yourself and your health

You look forward to having a restful sleep every night.

You believe in yourself.

You can do it.

Longer Pause

Stop Smoking with Self Hypnosis

You can use this process anytime when you are sitting in a chair. You do not have to listen to the whole recording to do this. You only have to know this process and you can self-hypnotize yourself at any time.

Begin this process by finding a comfortable place where you feel relaxed. Practice what I am saying in your mind as if you are doing this.

Pause

I am now sitting or lying here, with my feet side by side and my hands resting loosely. My head is supported, and I'm aware of all the sounds around me, however, they don't disturb me because for the next thirty minutes or so there is absolutely nothing at all for me to do but relax and let go.

Pause

As I begin to relax and listen to the sound of my voice, I know that from time to time my mind may get distracted, but that's fine. It's fine because right now, there is nothing else on my mind, I'm nothing but relaxed, and even if my mind begins to think of other, unpleasant thoughts, the words that I speak will penetrate deeply into my subconscious mind. Soon, my words will become my thoughts, and my thoughts become my new reality because I've made a conscious decision to become a non-smoker. I have made that decision and I intend to stick by it as I don't want to let myself down.

I'm aware of the weight and the shape of my feet and my legs. My feet are becoming so heavy, so heavy and so comfortably relaxed, so heavy and comfortable they just don't want to move. My feet now feel as heavy as lead, like two lead weights and they just don't want to move at all.

Longer Pause

My eyes are also becoming heavy along with my feet, my eyes are drifting so hard that they just want to close. They feel like onion skins, their layers are so heavy yet so comfortable. I feel so relaxed that when I close my eyes I'm aware of patterns of light filtering through my closed lids - the patterns of light; perhaps the colours like orange, pink even red. My eyes are becoming heavier and heavier, but I'm so comfortably relaxed they just don't want to open at all.

Pause

As I notice the heaviness on my lids, my hands and arms are relaxing more and more. I'm noticing the warmth in the palms of my hands, it is a lovely warm feeling, that tingling feeling in the palms of my hands and the heaviness is spreading from my fingertips up to the top of my shoulders.

It is making me comfortably tired and relaxes that I just want to drift away to a more comfortable place. This feeling is just so serene that it makes my whole body comfortable and makes me want to drift far away. It is taking me down to a wonderful place, the place I feared the most, it is taking myself deep inside me.

Pause

In the creative part of my subconscious mind, I have so many rooms, I can explore wherever I choose to. It was my conscious decision to become healthy again and that's one of the reasons that I have stopped smoking. Now onwards, I'm going to treat my body like it's a new day because I've had enough of abusing my body, filling my lungs with black smoke, tar, nicotine, and all the poisons contained in cigarettes. Starting today, I decide to be healthy, I want to breathe clean air and go back to my natural state.

Pause

I now realize that I wasn't always a smoker, there was once a wonderful time when I didn't even think about cigarettes, and I intend to back to those times. I want to recapture the feelings of health and vitality, of feeling clean and even disliking that stale unpleasant smell on those around me who smoked.

Longer Pause

I can recall how people looked silly to me when they were breathing in fumes into their own body and then breathing them out like silly children dicing with death. They seemed like they were taunting death and were saying, come and get me if you dare.

Now when I look back I think to myself, was I one of those people? Was I also behaving in a childish manner thinking that I was immortal?

Pause

I have done my research and now I know all the facts about smoking and until now I was choosing to ignore them, but not anymore. As I'm becoming more conscious now of how I treat my body, how could I have done that to me? It's never too late, but I won't put it off a moment longer, I'm a non-smoker now and I have decided that's all I need.

Pause

Going ahead, I might face some difficult moments, but I'm prepared for them, that's how much focused I'm. I'm willing to pay the price to stay determined because it is very hard to resist.

I have a very strong will, I will not fall for temporary temptations because I have my consciousness, that conscious mind has decided to be a non- smoker I'm not weak-willed - I'm me - I'm a strong person with a will and a mind of my own and that makes me proud.

Longer Pause

No more sneaking around to smoke cigarettes when other non-smokers are around, that part of my life is long gone, I'm conscious of the stale unpleasant smell of tobacco on people who smoke, and I notice it on their clothes, on their hair, on their breath and even on the skin of people who smoke. I'm glad that I don't smell dirty anymore, I'm so proud of myself because I did it.

I did it all by myself, no one else but me. It's such a wonderful feeling to be free of that old addiction of the mind. I'm now free from all the addictions and I'm fine.

I'm going to remember some happy memories of a time when I felt so proud and confident. As that memory begins to resurface, I'll take a couple of deep, refreshing breaths, and touch my earlobe with my hand to remind myself of how good I feel.
(Pause for a moment to allow a memory to come forward, and then touch the earlobe with hand).

Longer Pause

I can feel wonderful anytime I want to, I have all the confidence that I need to succeed, and if the thought of a cigarette enters my mind, I'll pause and take a couple of deep, refreshing breaths, and touch my earlobe with my hand. This will allow all those good feelings to come back to me anytime I want.

I'm now going to double the joy by squeezing my earlobe and by counting to five. I'm slowly lifting my hand and I'm squeezing my earlobe meanwhile I take some deep breaths continuing to count 1...2...3...4...5

Pause

I'm going to the creative part of my subconscious mind to explore those rooms, and in each one of those rooms are associations that I have with smoking. One of the rooms may involve smoking whilst talking to friends and I'm going into that room to get a sense of talking to my friends without a cigarette.

Instead of smoking, I'll take a couple of deep, refreshing breaths, while squeezing my earlobe and counting to five in my head. Those good feelings will break any association with smoking whilst talking to friends.

Pause

There is another room which also contains an association with smoking; it is after a heavy meal or with a drink. I'm going into that room to get a sense of finishing a meal or a drink without a cigarette, instead of smoking I'll take a couple of deep, refreshing breaths, squeeze my earlobe and count to five in my head and those good feelings will break any association with smoking.

Longer Pause

I will continue this process and I will search every room to break all my old associations with smoking. I will replace them with my new anchor and when I'm done with all the rooms, I will go for another round and then finally come back to the present time. While coming back, I will bring the determination and motivation that I need to succeed. I open my eyes feeling refreshingly alert and happy to be a non-smoker. All sensations of heaviness will leave my body as it returns to normal conscious awareness.

The Time Distortion Method

You are deeply relaxed, and the suggestions that you are now going to hear are going to have a lasting impact on your subconscious mind. You will keenly listen to every word I say even if your mind wanders sometimes. Right now, nothing else matters, nothing is more important than this beautiful relaxed feeling that you are experiencing.

Pause

At this point, you don't care about anything in this world, you understand that nobody wants anything, nobody needs anything and there is absolutely nothing at all for you to do except relax and let go. You just want to enjoy the feelings that are being generated within you.

Pause

Your eyes are beginning to feel heavy and sleepy, you could move but you just can't be bothered to, and you know how it is when you're just drifting off to sleep, your body sometimes makes an involuntary movement before letting go.

Your mind can wander away, the images can float into your mind and it's as though you become immersed in those images and dreams take over. When you are awake, you're well-rested, completely refreshed, and ready to begin a new day.

Longer Pause

What about those bad dreams? Where do they go? If you think of them as soon as you wake up, then you may remember elements of the dream. If the dream was vivid, you may remember every detail of it and only to forget at a later time.

The memory of those dreams remains in your subconscious mind, at an unconscious level that we surely won't recall every single dream that we ever had. Those dreams that seemed to last for so long, but in reality, were each just a few minutes short.

Pause

It is just as it is in hypnosis. We can travel forward, backward, or even sideways in our dreams where we're someone else completely. As you continue to listen to my voice, you are falling asleep.

My voice will be guiding you to a special sort of sleep, where you are not asleep but you are also not awake. You can hear my voice but your mind is just wandering off to its special thoughts that are led by things you unconsciously process.

Longer Pause

I would like to suggest that you experience a wonderful dream in your sleep, so go forward in time to six months from now where you're in a beautiful garden bordered with a mixture of colourful flowers and herbs that send out their perfume into the warm summer air. The air is still and birds are singing sweet songs in the trees.

There is a huge archway in your garden that is covered in jasmine and a little path leading through to a lovely ornamental pond with a rockery and a waterfall. You can hear the sound of the water hitting those rocks and splashing softly into the pond.

Pause

You realize how beautiful this place is and it is even better now because your sense of smell has improved, and the fragrance of your favourite flowers or herbs wafts under your nose. Imagine the smell of your favourite perfume, breathe slowly but deeply, and allow yourself to relax even more deeply.

Surprisingly, it's been more than six months since you smoked but you haven't missed it all. You have always wondered what it would like to be to stop smoking; you created this narrative in your head that it may not be as easy as it was, but now that you are experiencing it, you feel that you've never felt better in your life before.

You are only thinking about smoking now because I mentioned it, but the rest of the time it's a thing of the past, for you, it's a bad habit that you used to have.

Longer Pause

Six months have gone by, your health is regained, and you have more energy and self-respect. You feel cleaner, fresher, healthier, and fitter, as life is wonderful now for you. When you see someone else smoking you wonder how they could do that to themselves, putting that filthy thing into their mouth, inhaling the smoke, and the tar into their lungs. It seems pointless to you even though you know that sometime in the past you once did the same thing, but that was before you discovered a better way.

I want you to hold these good feelings right there, and tell yourself that, "I haven't smoked for six months, so why should I now". Now, remember the garden of perfume, the beauty of nature, and living in harmony with your mind, your body, and your spirit of love. Imagine holding on to those good feelings in your hand and clasping them in your fist if you like because the feelings are becoming so strong that you want to hold onto them forever.

Longer Pause

Now relax, as I'm bringing you back in time to (name the present date) and you're still feeling good. You clasp your hand again and tell yourself once more, "I haven't smoked for six months, so why should I now".

When you wake up from this hypnotic dream you will completely believe that you have not smoked for six months, and you will think to yourself that you don't want to smoke ever again.

All other memories remain intact, but the fact is you truly feel as though you have not smoked for six whole months, why should you now. You will keep this belief to yourself because you know in your heart that you're a non-smoker and you hold that good feeling right there in your hand.

You could be anything you want to, so you are a non-smoker now. You've already been a non-smoker for six whole months, so it doesn't matter if you know that, on one hand, you had smoked in the past and on the other hand you have all those wonderful feelings that you gained in hypnosis from traveling six months into your beautiful future.

Longer Pause

When you wake up, you will have an inner belief that you have been a non-smoker for six months, so there's no point in starting again now. You're over it, smoking is a dead-end for you, you finished smoking before it finished you, and now you're free. You are completely in control of your habits.

Pause

What your subconscious mind can conceive, your conscious mind can achieve, like your belief that you've already stopped smoking grows stronger and stronger every day. Since you've already stopped smoking, there's no point in falling in the rabbit hole again.

Remain in hypnosis for another few minutes whilst you enjoy these wonderful feelings, just enjoy being here in your special place and notice how this place becomes a part of you. This is a wonderful place which you can visit again whenever you wish to, and all with the power of your mind.

Learning to Relax

Let's learn how to relax yourself every time you feel stressed.

You are now going to take in a deep breath, hold it for a few seconds and then exhale and try to relax.

Pause

Take in a second breath in your full capacity. And while you exhale, allow the stress persisting inside your mind to release. Allow it to let go.

Pause

For a third time, take in the third deep breath, try holding it as long as you can and as you exhale during that time, ask your mind to rest by saying "Relax now".

Consequently, always try to relax whenever you face a stressful situation. So whenever you feel stressed in the future just remember to follow the above steps, take three deep breaths, and at the end while you exhale quietly tell yourself the appellation "Relax now".

Longer Pause

You are now progressing towards developing a fresh way to relax. You are not concerned anymore about the stress of the past and now all you have decided is to relax and be peaceful. There is no space for stress in your life. Unhappiness, anger, irritation don't exist in your life. This not only hampers your physical health but disturbs emotional equilibrium which you don't want in your life.

From now on, follow a peaceful, calm life. It's the time to react in a controlled way in whatever you do because health is most precious.

Pause

Modifying your habits, changing the way of your action are your new habits now. These steps are for your wellbeing. I will give some more positive recommendations and by following it, you will experience that your life is stress-free and you will feel more relieved and relaxed in your daily routine.

The situations that stressed you in the past will no longer bother you. Moreover, this suggestion will make your lifestyle calm and composed, you will feel more cheerful. Appreciating your life is all that you need to think about from now.

Pause

The human mind is really complex. My first suggestion for you is that our mind may have some dim view, negative mindset, lack of confidence, and you might be thinking that your future may be worse but now you are going to respond to this in a positive way by saying the word "Stop". I will tell you this again to make it more comprehensible. Each and every time you start having negative thoughts, gloomy outlook, you need to tell your mind to STOP.

Longer Pause

As soon as you command the word Stop, your bad thoughts will drop out of sight making your mind stress-free and it will let your mind welcome more clear, confident positive thoughts and will replace the negative thoughts making you believe in what's happening instead of what has happened.

Pause

From this day on, no matter whatever makes you stressed about any state of affairs which is not in your control or even if you imagine any uncertain situation, you will no longer get anxious about it and will accept whatever the situation brings to you. You will realize that accepting reality is a very important key.

Pause

Your mind is ready now to tackle any situation and you can now easily formulate the solution whatever the consequences are. You should act first before thinking about the result. Working out on your problems instead of worrying about it will let your mind free.

You are over and done with worrying, it is no more a part of your life. It is now replaced by a relaxing and peaceful mind.

Pause

At present, your thoughts, emotion, sentiment are in your control. You have control over them rather than they have over you.

We are noticing something very interesting, you have become an actor rather than a Re-actor. Let me elaborate on this, whenever you are in a stressful situation you are the one who is going to make the final decision on your actions in a particular situation. Now you choose to react calmly, with a positive attitude. You are completely under control.

Pause

Now just for a second, I would like to bring your attention to your breathing cycle. Start concentrating on your breathing, breathe in and breathe out, at the very moment when you start feeling that you have exhaled all the air, you can prepare yourself for another breathe count till 25 in silence, take a second breath now and it doesn't need to be a deep breath instead it can be a normal one.

Now start your breathing count up to 24. After that, take another breath for a duration that appears normal to you and then breathe out, counting up to 23 and continue counting from beginning to the end.

Longer Pause

At the very moment when you take your final deep breath just exhale out and count number one, you are now going to open your eyes. As you open your eyes you feel more insouciant, relaxed, and comfortable in all the senses. This feeling will make you refreshed more than ever.

Longer Pause

As I explain this to you, you continue counting each one of your breaths, focusing on the flow of your breathing and how it is filling your body and leaves. You will now feel every sensation. As you go more in-depth, you will start feeling more refreshed and relaxing. Once you open your eyes you will feel astonishing in every possible way.

Here begins your journey of quitting smoking. You are determined to give up smoking and this determination is going to lead you to success. And the road leading you to quit smoking will eventually relax your mind. Yes, you heard that right, you can now calm down and relax, now walk away from all this and make the most of it to feel serene and relaxed.

Pause

This is the time you have chosen for yourself so drop everything and walk away leaving all painful experiences behind and just be relaxed. Allow yourself to relax thoroughly, the more you will feel relaxed the more you will be progressing towards your goal of quitting smoking. You are here because of your strong and inclined determination to end this deadly habit of smoking.

And the reason for choosing this session is not due to the influence of others, you are here because of your absolute determination. You see today as a day which will make you a non-smoker for your whole life.

Longer Pause

Your life will not be in control of that small white piece of paper containing tobacco. You are the one who has taken full control over your urges for smoking. The first step has been already taken
here. You are now ready to transform into a non-smoker. You have to stick to your decision and at the end of this session, you will achieve the objective and come out of this session as a non-smoker.

Pause

Smoking will never be part of your future life, it will be eradicated once and forever and you will not smoke in any circumstances.

This obnoxious habit will be your past now.

This will be a brand-new rise of you and your current life as a non-smoker will never let you smoke again. So as the clock is ticking at the moment, imagine yourself as a non-smoker who has stopped smoking and the one who will by no means ever smoke again.

Currently, you are a non-smoker and have this ability to control your urge for smoking, even if you are surrounded by people who are smokers.

You know how to cherish your life even without smoking, you are aware of all pros and cons. Moreover, your life is happier and healthier now as a non-smoker.

As a fact of the matter, it makes no difference to you whether you are in the office, home, all alone, or with friends, your mind is in your control. Whether you are eating, driving, doing some tasks, or relaxing, solely that seems much more delightful as a non-smoker.

Pause

This feeling is phenomenal, your life is without any stress, and healthier. With each passing day, you will breathe without constraints.

Quitting this habit of smoking will not only be beneficial for your health but it will help you gain more confidence also.

Just make this confidence rush inside your spirit and mind, enable it to flow within you right now at this moment. You have to comprehend that you are a non-smoker with this confidence that you have attained, you need to live life.

It is not easy to quit such a habit, but you have conquered this journey very easily with your enthusiasm. At this moment you are filled with self-confidence and positiveness in your mind.

Longer Pause

It is essential to remember that to carry off anything worthwhile in your life you have to give your best shot. And it takes even more effort to continue to be a non-smoker that is 100% effort, 100% to succeed, and 100% to your dedication.

This commitment of yours is not made to anyone else but your true self and you are always going to give 100% to accomplish your target.

Presently you have stopped smoking, you became a non-smoker willingly and you will never smoke again in your life. As time passes your inclination, desire, promptness towards your health is strengthened with greater purpose.

Pause

Besides being a non-smoker, you have established a new positive habit, which is not only going to help you in the present but also for your entire life.

This moment forth, this feeling will be in a more striking manner than ever. You have exceeded in mastering this good habit of giving up on smoking. Instead of that, you have developed a habit of having water at proper duration which is beneficial for your health. This water will taste much more fresh and tonic. This refreshing water will fulfill your desire like it has never done before.

At the present moment, you must have started observing that whenever you think about the water you start feeling thirsty, there is no need to worry this is just your body's natural reflex.

Longer Pause

At this moment you are aware that you are not a smoker anymore, and filled with positive energy. This energy, liveliness will be used for other good deeds in your life. You are now realizing that you are feeling more positive by attending this session and it's guiding you through a happy life, you are experiencing intensified feelings about yourself. You have started utilizing your power in better habits like going to morning walk, you might be parking your car a little bit further so that you can walk for some more distance till you reach your office to do more physical work.

Adapting new healthy eating habits is your new hobby. These additional habits are instinctual by-products of becoming healthier. They are all the result of your true determination and will power.

Smoking Cessation II

As you are becoming more comfortable and relaxed, you will find your mind wandering here and there occasionally by drifting off in the direction it wants, but you know that it's okay. There is nothing big for you to do right now, there is no place to go, no problems to solve, nothing to do but to relax and let go, so relax your mind and let go of your worries.

Pause

As you let go, you become more aware of my voice, perhaps not consciously, but subconsciously you will listen to every word I say, and soon enough, my words will become your thoughts. Your thoughts will start to generate a whole new way of thinking, feeling, and will start being there for you.

Longer Pause

You have been having some unwanted troublesome thoughts for a while now and those thoughts preyed on your mind and made you feel like you are emotionally and physically ill. But count on changing the narrative, the changes will happen quite soon not because I say so and certainly not because of any miracle or even this hypnotic experience, but because you have decided to change. You have decided who you are, you took your control back and now, you alone are in charge of you.

Pause

It took a long time for experts like psychologists, doctors, and other people working in the field of neurological disorders to find that people don't have bad thoughts because they feel bad, but it is more often because it's the other way around. They constantly think that something wrong is going to happen which generates some uncomfortable emotions, and a feeling of general discomfort in them.

Considering everything, I have decided to show you the simplest technique in the world that will allow you to eliminate all those unwanted thoughts once and for all. You are going to use the 'thought stopping' technique together with your anchor to reinforce what you're learning which will double the effect of what you say to yourself to get rid of those thoughts.

Longer Pause

Let me explain the technique first and then we will go through some examples so we can strengthen your knowledge of how to apply it.

Whenever a bad thought comes into your mind I want you to *(if you are right-handed, then use it otherwise vice versa of the instruction)* use the middle three fingers of your right hand to gently slap over the middle three fingers of the left hand and say the word 'Stop'. When you say 'Stop', you are telling yourself that this thought is not true and you are not accepting the thought to be real.

To enable yourself to believe what you're saying, we will now go through one or two examples of typical negative thoughts.

Most people are misguided by their past mistakes and some toxic people around them. They think that they are bad people because they made a mistake or something went wrong in their life. You must have experienced such an occasion where you opened your mouth to say something and immediately regretted it after it came out of your mouth. You then go on to beat yourself up about it for ages afterward. Strangely enough, the more thought you give about that situation, the more power you are giving to it, it becomes stronger and you feel worse than you were feeling before.

Pause

If you took time to reflect and held that thought up to the light soon afterward and saw it for what it was, you would have realized that it was just a slip of the tongue or an inadvertent response. Does that make it your mistake? Does that make you a bad person? If someone else was in the same position, would you have punished them as much as you are punishing yourself? Exactly, I don't think so.

After a quick evaluation of this situation, you have decided that you're not bad after all; you slap yourself gently on the left hand and say the word 'Stop' to yourself. The exact words will be "Stop, this thought is not true and I am not accepting this thought to be real".

Pause

For instance, you are preparing for a test or perhaps awaiting the results of a medical examination, all sorts of things will go through your mind, like, "What if I fail?", "What if the result is negative?", "Is this the end of the world?". Hold those thoughts up to the light and see them clearly for what they are. If you fail an exam, it's not the end of the world; you can still prepare yourself better for another one. If it's a medical situation, your chances of recovery will be higher if you approach it with a positive mind, and the chance of your results being in your favor will be more than 50-50, so now slap yourself gently on the left hand and say the word 'Stop' to yourself. You will say, "Stop, this thought is not true and I am not accepting this thought to be real"

Longer Pause

You will learn to examine and evaluate your negative thoughts rapidly by slapping the thoughts out of your mind, you will realize that after just a short while that you can eliminate them instantly by using this six finger technique by saying the word 'Stop' to yourself.

You will say "Stop, this thought is not true and I am not accepting this thought to be real". It will go away if you follow this; it is as easy and as simple as that.

You are going to find yourself using this method more often to clean out those toxic thoughts, and the more you use these methods, the more strength you give to a positive outcome, soon you will realize that you are eliminating negative thoughts easily and rapidly because they are losing their power over you. They begin to diminish and you find yourself to be more positive with healthy thoughts which make you feel happier, calmer, and more confident than ever before.

These suggestions will be solidly embedded in your subconscious mind and will grow stronger day by day, they will grow firmer by the day and stronger by the hour and solid by the minute.

Hypnosis Benefits Script

A lot of people have been able to quit smoking under hypnosis. It is a heightened state of awareness that allows you to have easy access to what resides in your subconscious mind.

The hypnotic state is also called as trance and this is also called as the state of suspended disbelief. In this relaxed state of mind, you are able to let go of what your conscious mind thinks. In fact, the conscious takes a back seat and this also happens when you are reading an interesting book or looking outside the window for a longer period of time. Hypnosis is a pure relaxation and this audio only allows you to get into that state of mind.

And in this state of mind, you do not want a cigarette and you will continue to listen to the sound of my voice.

You get into the hypnotic state every now and then without consciously knowing it. And some of the everyday hypnosis examples are

You are in an elevator and as you continue to see the numbers go down, you know that you are going down and down knowing that each number down means each floor down…like

10, 9….8….7……6….5….4…

The door opens and you follow the people who are with you and move out of the elevator until you realize that you are on a wrong floor. And, you then wait for another elevator to come so that you can take that and reach the ground floor.

And, the other elevator comes and you step into it…and it starts to further go down and this time you are focused on the numbers and ….4….3…2….1….and 0.

Similarly, the experience of driving, when you are driving and you cross many traffic signals, crossroads, go through exits, thinking about something at work or listening to your favorite track and then you reach the destination without even realizing that it took you 30 minutes..

Or when you read an interesting book, you imagine the story in your mind and pay minimal attention to what is happening around you…because the conscious is aware of everything around you but does not interfere in you and your book. Because it takes a back seat.

And you have created the same state now…you are deeply relaxed where you are focused on the sound of my voice and your conscious mind has taken a back seat…and whatever is being said now goes directly into your subconscious mind…which is a powerhouse of knowledge and can help you change all the habits…which includes smoking too.

This is perhaps the light state or deep state of trance, it does not matter, because any state feels good. Isn't it?

A lot of people smoke as they believe that it helps them kill boredom, relax, and make them stress free. And, that is absolutely wrong. Smoking increases stress and impedes relaxation. And now you know of the trance state or hypnotic state…and how it can change any habit.

Longer Pause

You are good at inducing this state anytime and with self-hypnosis, you can direct your mind to change anything that serves no purpose.

In this state, you will be reprogramming your subconscious mind to set goals for better health. You will be letting go of a habit and making new choices as if you are cleaning an overflowing drawer of your end table.

And, I wonder if you could imagine cleaning the drawer that is full of clutter and how it is affecting your mood.

Pause

When you open the drawer, you notice old papers, filled diaries, pencils, non-working pens, wrappers of candies, some expired medicines, some accessories that are of no use….

Longer Pause

Take all of them out and put them in the trash can…and feel how you feel about the clean drawer…

Pause

As you notice the clean drawer, you notice you have now new space to put in things that are important for you…that do good to you…

Similarly, your subconscious is clean now to take in new information and the new information is that you are a non-smoker. And, you are motivated to stay a non-smoker.

Being a non-smoker makes you powerful, brave, and happier.

You take multivitamins including B complex and vitamin c regularly. You drink lots of water throughout the day to keep yourself hydrated. You pay more attention to your body and health. You love yourself even more now.

And it is so easy to stay as a non-smoker continuing to feel amazing about yourself and taking pride in it.

With every passing day, your will is becoming stronger and stronger as you are becoming even more relaxed and calmer.

Pause

You are a non-smoker and you enjoy being one.

You inspire others and tell them how you overcame it.

It is all about taking the decision, diverting the thoughts of cigarettes, consciously getting rid of the packs, and knowing that you need to live a fulfill your life.

You love your life and family immensely and you are an active non-smoker and a passive non-smoker.

Longer Pause

You stop yourself from standing and sitting with people who smoke.

And, if at all anyone offers you a cigarette, with high self-esteem and assertiveness, you know exactly what you need to say.

You straightforwardly say NO to them.

And, in no way you cannot make the same mistake which you perhaps made many times in the past because it is a waste of time and energy by quitting it for a few days and then going back to it.

You are very sure of your decision and you know it feels like to be a non-smoker and a smoker.

Silky Breathing

Continue to breathe and allow yourself to go deeper and deeper with every breath you take. And, I wonder if you can count your breath and as you do so and exhale…allow every little tension in your body go out…

As you continue to breathe, imagine, visualize, or feel your breath to be soft and smooth like silk. This feels like breathing in soft silk like breath…smooth and soft.

Pause

Perhaps you give it a color to the soft and silky breath…the most relaxing and calming color and as you imagine that, you allow that color to move into your face and head…that spreads down to the back of your head and neck, going further down to your spine, reaching upper back, middle, and lower back…

And imagine giving it a nice smell…a flower or your favorite perfume's fragrance. Whatever you like, give it a beautiful fragrance and imagine that fragrant silk moving down your hips, back of your thighs, calves, ankles, heels, and feet….

Pause

As you continue to breathe, you imagine the fragrant soft silk moving up into your shins, knees, thighs, torso, chest and shoulders…

Now, imagine it moving it into your lungs as you continue to feel the silk and smell its beautiful fragrance.

Longer Pause

And perhaps now the silk has a flavor too. And, the flavor that you like that enhances the experience…

Allow yourself to inhale the beautiful fragrance, color, and flavor of this silk and maybe now give it a sound…

Longer Pause

A sound that relaxes you…it could be a sound of the waves, your favorite tune, or anything that comes to your mind now. It could even me a vibration….

Pause

As you continue to breathe, you breathe in the sound, the fragrance, the flavor, the color, the feel…of the silk…

That's right.

It almost feels like a beautiful silk sheet all around you that feels so comfy and relaxing…and imagine this silky sheet becoming bigger and bigger and covering you from all sides…

Pause

You feel so comfy having it around you…you feel safe and comfortable. It wraps you and soothes every emotion and thought.
This is now your sheet of comfort and you can imagine it having on and around you every time you feel stressed in future.

Pause

It relaxes your feelings and thoughts as it carries the calming sound, your favorite fragrance, the relaxing color, the silky touch, and the flavor wrapping you from all sides…

And all thoughts regarding cigarettes simply melt away…would you like the thought of smoke and the smell of smoke to remain in this silky sheet?

I know your answer is No…and perhaps it would be the same for me…

All the thoughts about smoking leave your silky sheet and go far away from you…

Pause

Imagine going further deep into this comforting state of relaxation and allow your subconscious mind to open to the suggestions

And repeat in your mind after me…

I love being healthy (4-5 seconds pause)

I have taken charge of my health (4-5 seconds pause)

I love myself and my body fully (4-5 seconds pause)

Pause

Now imagine that the corner of the silky sheet is between your fingers and palm and you tighten your fist to feel it better…

And as you do so, you feel the softness and silkiness between the fingers and palm…

This is a reminder that every time you need to feel calm and relaxed, you simply have to tighten your fist and you will enter this same state of relaxation

Especially, when you crave a cigarette, all you have to do is only tighten your fist and the thoughts about it will leave you and go far away…

Pause

I wonder if you can now imagine a tall clear glass of water. It is cool and clean…

Imagine having a sip and feel the water go down your throat, reaching the chest, and your stomach…

Having more water has many benefits as it flushes out the toxins, helps in losing weight, gives more mental clarity, keeps you alert…and makes you productive.

You can enjoy the benefits of water by having at least 8 glasses of cool and clean water everyday…

Longer Pause

Perhaps it also cleanses you of the thoughts about the cigarettes.

Imagine having a tall glass of water now and notice how instantly you feel relaxed, calm, and positive…

Every time you take a sip, you feel stronger about staying non-smoker.

This only means, that water replaces cigarettes.

Pause

The more water you consume, the stronger you feel about staying a non-smoker.

That's right.

Now, let's come back to the silky breathing…imagine breathing in your favorite fragrance, the calming color, the melodious sound, the soft touch, and your favorite flavor…

Pause

Imagine the silky sheet all around you. You feel so calm and relaxed…that you want to just sleep and drift further into an even better state of relaxation.

Staying Committed Script

Notice how your breathing is, soft and fragrant…like silk.

And as you continue to listen to me and enjoy this beautiful state of relaxation, I wonder if you can imagine yourself in a beautiful open meadow.

The grass in lush green and moist…and imagine it beneath your feet. Feel it underneath and look around. The surroundings are beautiful, the weather is perfect, it is breezy, and the sunshine is warm and crisp.

Longer Pause

You can feel the breeze against your skin and as you feel that, you notice tall trees in front of you that are swaying with the wind…and this meadow is a place to learn.

In the front, you notice a beautiful white path with dry leaves on it. You decide to walk on it and as you move forward, you notice hearing your own footsteps…

And moving forward means moving towards your future…

What's behind is the past…your past where you experienced a lot as a child or a teenager or an adult…learnt many lessons.

And in front, you have a life that you have not experienced really but where you are right now, with all the decisions you have made, you know you will be able to make your future better…and decide on better things..

Isn't it…

Longer Pause

You keep walking and reach a place where the path splits into two. One path goes to the left and the other path goes to the right…you are the fork in the path.

Allow your mind to rest here.

You have a choice to make now…each path has its own possibilities…

The left path is almost like the path as your past…with same lifestyle, same life, same habits…

The right path has new possibilities with better health, a new and healthier lifestyle, stronger and clear mind, better sleep, and much more…

You are at the deciding point and as you stand at the fork, you know that you have to make a commitment to being a non-smoker. To stay as a non-smoker for the rest of your life. You want to be healthier and happier…living a fulfilling life and having a longer life.

This is a decision for life. So, you decide to walk both paths before you take that decision.

Longer Pause

You step on the path to your left…and start to walk on it…and the life here is pretty much the same. You are smoking, coughing, having breathing issues. You have the feelings of guilt about smoking, you want to quit but unable to. You are struggling to quit, you feel stressed, and tired.

Many years down the line, you see yourself as getting older before time, it seems the cigarettes have taken a toll on your skin. You are getting wrinkles before time, the skin looks dehydrated, you cough most of the times, and your body feels fatigued.

The family members love you a lot, however, they feel disappointed in you. They wish if you could quit smoking and live joyously with them for a long time.

You know that the life will remain the same on this path…the path of constant struggle, guilt, and disappointment.

Now, imagine going back to the fork.

Pause

You are back at the fork in the path…and because you need to make the decision today about commitment, you decide to walk the path to your right…to see how the future will be if you chose this path.

Take the right path now…

And as you step on it, you feel the cool breeze against your face…the air here is clean. You are breathing in fresh and clean air…few steps down the path, you notice living a healthier life…

Everything here is positive and you feel confident and calm. There is a sense of freedom and lightness…you are energetic, active, and healthy.

The friends and family here admire you and get inspired by the choices you have made. Further down the path, you notice yourself living an amazing life with your family and friends. Life is really good here.

You have a clearer mind and a fitter body. The older you get, the healthier you get, your skin looks young and feel energetic, positive, and much happier.

This life lifts you up in every way…

Longer Pause

Now come back to the fork.

Pause

And as you stand at the fork, you now know how each path looks in the future and you now have to make a choice and decide on the path that will make you happier, positive, and healthier. So, whether you want to live a free, healthy and happy life or live a tiring, unhealthy, and mediocre life, is your choice.

Look at the paths again as you stand at the fork. And as you stand here, you reach your inner wisdom and get guidance.

Longer Pause

What is it that you want to do?

Allow your mind to prepare and imagine that there is a panel in your brain that takes care of urges, desires, cravings, habits, thoughts, and emotions…

Reach that place in your mind NOW.

Notice the panel and it has many switches and pulleys. I wonder if you find a switch for cigarettes. If yes, switch it off immediately.

That's right..

And, now that it is switched off, you know that the thoughts pertaining to cigarettes wont enter your mind. And you will never have to worry about stopping the cravings or diverting your mind. The cigarette switch is completely OFF.

And, now that it is turned off, it's going to be easier and effortless to choose the right path.

The path to your right is the right path…isn't it?

Step on it now.

Pause

And as you step on the path of healthier life, you feel proud of yourself to have taken this decision. Life feels amazing her. The world here looks so much better. You are free, happier, positive, and healthier. You breathe clean and fresh air, your lungs are perfect, your skin glows, you look much younger than your age.

You are a non-smoker.

As you continue to walk on the path, you notice that after few years, you have become emotionally and mentally stronger. The health has improved manifold. The decision of quitting smoking has added many years to your life.

The life here is amazing. You have better relationships with people. People love you for your strong will power. You have been inspiring them.

You are so grateful that you made the decision long ago and are sticking to it. You are committed to being a non-smoker.

You are a non-smoker

It is so easy to stay as a non-smoker

And it is very important for you to stay as a non-smoker.

You are happy being a non-smoker because the results are phenomenal. You love yourself fully and completely. You love your body, your health, your life, and the decision you made.

These suggestions will go deeper into your subconscious mind…with every passing moment…

That's right.

Get rid of the Compulsion Script

As you continue to listen to me and take each breath, you are drifting further down in a deeper state of mind that allows you to be more attentive to what I am saying.

As you relax, you feel so proud and confident about making this positive change in your life. The change that will give you great health and allow you to live a fulfilling life.

Every word I say causes you to embrace health and reject smoking or cigarettes. Every time you listen to this audio, it reinforces the fact that you are a non-smoker 1000 times. You are free from the old nasty and smelly habit of yours. Every part of your being enjoys being free and breathing in clean and fresh air.

Pause

Your organs are thanking you for making this important decision.

You are in control of your choices and you are celebrating this freedom and are proud of the decision you have made.

The part of you perhaps thought of smoking and the other part is this who is listening to me, who wants to live as a non-smoker.

Pause

And you have already spoken to that part that he will be your friend to keep you stay focused on the life time goal of staying a non-smoker always. You are not going to be the slaves of the old habit and it feels amazing to be in control and free.

You are in charge of your choices, decisions, and behaviours. You have decided to choose a life that is healthier giving you better health, longer life, clear throat, better skin, and fresher breath. And there is no stench of tobacco in your hands and hair.

With no smoke smell in your hands, hair, and clothes, you appear much more attractive to your friends, family, and your partner.

Pause

You also notice your teeth getting cleaner and gums becoming healthier. You are totally free of tobacco and this leads to a happy and healthier life. You are a non smoker for the rest of your life. No amount of tension or stress can let you pick up smoking. You have better ways to cope up with stress or tension that does not harm your body.

You had come to a fork in the path and you saw yourself living a healthy life and decided on living a healthy smoke free life. You also saw how the path with smoking looked and felt like.

Pause

And every part of you, have together decided on take the path of non-smoking. The road you have already taken is the road of tobacco free life.

Anytime, there is a faintest thought about cigarette in your mind, you simply reject it. You get reminded of the path you have chosen and you reinforce the fact in your mind that you have chosen this path, you take responsibility of it. And this gives you immense confidence and the feeling of significance that you have been able to bring positive changes to your life.

Pause

If you happen to be around smokers, you feel as if you have never smoked and the smell in the air causes your mind to reject smoking, which is 1000 times more powerful. There is a sense of pride you feel every time you reject a cigarette or reject a thought about it. The self-respect increases and you feel courage and strength in yourself.

You also think about how much money have you wasted in the past on cigarettes. And, how much you can save now with this decision. Perhaps, use that money to enjoy better things in life. Maybe a vacation, gym membership, learning courses, so on and so forth.

And, because you have chosen to be a non-smoker, you have created a new truth for you. This truth is planted in the deepest part of your being and guides your new life as a non-smoker.

Longer Pause

The truth is that you are a non-smoker. And, you keep hearing this in your mind every now and then. This may have many variations but the meaning would be same. You may hear statements like – I love to be a non-smoker, I am a non-smoker for life, I choose to be a non-smoker, I reject smoking. I think and feel like a non-smoker.

Your subconscious mind locks this new truth deep into the deepest part of you so that it becomes your reality and you live this truth in the real world.

Pause

The second new truth is: I have NO desire to smoke. I reject smoking subconsciously and consciously.

And this again goes deeper into your deepest part of your mind and becomes your reality.

The next truth is that Smoking is a thing of past. You have released all the smoking and all of that stays in the past as if it has been locked in the past. There is no way that it can come forward and be a part of your current life. Smoking is a thing of past. Your past holds all the effects of smoking. In this current time, you are a non-smoker.

Pause

The truth is: I have moved past my past. Smoking is a thing of past.

And, the next truth is again – I am a non-smoker. I am permanently free from smoking. And, this goes further deep into your subconscious mind. This makes you feel empowered, confident, and wise.

Pause

In this place of new truths, you are a non-smoker, you have a zero desire to smoke, smoking is a thing of past, and you are a non-smoker. You are free from smoking. You enjoy this freedom as a non-smoker. You love your health and love your body.

And these new truths lock themselves in your subconscious mind. You hear them always at the back of your mind, like a background music. Every time you hear each truth, you are all the more determined to stay focused on the journey of being a non smoker. These truths are unbreakable and unshakeable. This is your new reality and you choose to stay as a non-smoker for the rest of your life. Living healthily and happily.

And as I count down from 5 down to 1, these suggestions will go deeper into your subconscious mind.

Pause

Starting now at 5, going deeper at 4….further deep at 3….locking themselves in the deepest part of your subconscious mind….2……locked….1…..you are a non smoker..

Live a Smoke Free Life

And you continue to drift deeper and deeper into this relaxed state of mind and as you continue to drift, you begin to relax even more and enjoy the wonderful feeling of being at calm. And, everything is perfect right now.

Pause

All the stress and tensions have gone far away leaving you here feeling absolutely peaceful and relaxed. You are going with the flow as you continue to listen to each word I say. No one wants anything from you…and this makes you so much more relaxed that you can fully focus in here and now.

And, I want to say a big congratulations to you for making this wonderful decision to quit smoking and living your life in a healthier way. With the commitment you have made, you have shown yourself that you can do take great decisions in life for your health and live healthily.

Pause

We are going to use the same positive reinforcement now in this state of your mind so that it goes deeper into your subconscious mind and you continue to stay committed to yourself and continue to stay non-smoker for the rest of your life.

You are listening to me because you want to stay a non-smoker for the rest of your life and because you have already seen the effects of smoking. And it can have serious repercussions on your health later in life. And, because of this, you have already quit it and feel so proud of taking that decision.

Pause

From today on you look forward to having an amazing life where you give your health utmost priority. You see yourself in future as a healthy person enjoying all the good things in life. You have overcome an old habit of yours that did not do any good to you. And this only reinforces that you will continue to keep yourself healthy without any nicotine in your body.

And with every passing day, your old way of life fades away into a distant memory…as if you come out of a tunnel and is all brightness and sunshine all around you.

Pause

You are always conscious of the motivation and determination to stay healthy and keep your body clean, which ultimately makes you active, energetic, and happy.

You put good things in your mouth, things that give you nutrition and makes you go on without causing any bad effects to your body. And all these things include good food, lots of water, and healthy drinks. You eat healthy and you breathe in healthy air. And all of this is visible on your body and face in no time.

Perhaps you have already started to see the difference on your face and body. Perhaps your face has gotten clearer…

Longer Pause

You are very happy with the decision that you have made to live a healthier and happier life. This also include the feelings of pride and courage. You have been courageous to take that decision and stick to it and that gives you the feeling of pride. And these feelings grow deeper and deeper with every passing day and with every word I say.

You are aware that your actions have a direct influence on the friends and family. And the decision of quitting smoking is setting a great example for the people so that they also know that if you can do it then anyone can do it. And everyone looks upto you and talk about you to others. This way you are not only helping the people you know directly but also the people you do not know like the friends of your friends and family.

Pause

And when you think about your old life. You think that you were stupid to have smoked for so long and life seems so much better without cigarettes. You again feel relieved by knowing that you have taken a right decision to be happier, healthier, more active and inspiring.

Pause

You are free from all the unwanted habits and addiction and you are proud of it. You have a strong will power and your mind is committed to the decision and continue to stay committed because you love yourself a lot and in no way you can let damage yourself.

Affirmations

1. You are a non-smoker (7 seconds pause)
2. You breathe better (7 seconds pause)
3. You love your body and you take utmost care of it (7 seconds pause)
4. You look forward to living a smoke free life (7 seconds pause)
5. You hate cigarettes (7 seconds pause)
6. Cigarettes remind you of cancer and all the costs that come with it (7 seconds pause)
7. You enjoy being a non-smoker (7 seconds pause)
8. You love yourself unconditionally (7 seconds pause)
9. You save money as a non-smoker (7 seconds pause)
10. You love yourself (7 seconds pause)
11. You love your body (7 seconds pause)
12. You want to live a long life (7 seconds pause)
13. You want to enjoy the gifts of life (7 seconds pause)
14. You drink 8 to 10 glasses of water everyday (7 seconds pause)
15. You take care of your health everyday (7 seconds pause)
16. You love to exercise (7 seconds pause)
17. You sleep on time and take care of your sleep cycle (7 seconds pause)
18. Your skin improves with every passing day as a non-smoker (7 seconds pause)
19. Your skin glows with health and radiance (7 seconds pause)
20. You breathe fresh air (7 seconds pause)
21. You have more interesting things to do as a non-smoker (7 seconds pause)
22. You love being a non-smoker (7 seconds pause) (7 seconds pause)
23. You feel amazing as a non-smoker (7 seconds pause)
24. Your self love and self-appreciation has increased (7 seconds pause)
25. You respect your body, mind, and soul (7 seconds pause)
26. Everyday, you are feeling healthier and happier (7 seconds pause)
27. You prefer to breathe fresh air every day (7 seconds pause)
28. You choose to live as a non smoker (7 seconds pause)
29. You choose to not smoke and feel great about yourself (7 seconds pause)
30. You live a smoke free life (7 seconds pause)
31. Your lungs are feeling great with every passing day (7 seconds pause)
32. You love your freedom as a non-smoker (7 seconds pause)
33. You have a deep love for your body (7 seconds pause)
34. Your self-esteem improves as a non-smoker (7 seconds pause)
35. Your breathing has improved tremendously (7 seconds pause)
36. You are able to taste food better (7 seconds pause)
37. You are much calmer and relaxed as a non-smoker (7 seconds pause)
38. You are so happy to have given up smoking completely (7 seconds pause)
39. Your sleep cycle is getting better (7 seconds pause)
40. You sleep better and fall asleep faster (7 seconds pause)
41. You have taken charge of your health and body and that makes you feel amazing (7 seconds pause)
42. You are so happy as a non-smoker (7 seconds pause)

43. You are proud of yourself to have overcome nicotine addiction (7 seconds pause)
44. You are stronger than a cigarette (7 seconds pause)
45. You are the master of your mind (7 seconds pause)
46. You have control on your thoughts (7 seconds pause)
47. You are proud to have a healthy lifestyle (7 seconds pause)
48. You inspire people (7 seconds pause)
49. You breathe better (7 seconds pause)
50. You breathe fresh air (7 seconds pause)
51. You are stronger than any habit (7 seconds pause)
52. You can change habits easily (7 seconds pause)
53. You choose to live a healthy and happy life (7 seconds pause)
54. You overcome unhealthy habits easily (7 seconds pause)
55. You deserve an amazing life (7 seconds pause)
56. You are incredible and powerful (7 seconds pause)
57. You are positive and happier (7 seconds pause)
58. From now on, you are a permanent non-smoker (7 seconds pause)
59. Smoking is a thing of past (7 seconds pause)
60. You relax yourself easily when you are stressed (7 seconds pause)
61. You manage stress easily (7 seconds pause)
62. You don't let anything affect your life (7 seconds pause)
63. You are living a smoke free life (7 seconds pause)
64. Life is all good and healthy now (7 seconds pause)
65. You love yourself a lot (7 seconds pause)
66. Life is beautiful (7 seconds pause)
67. You love your body (7 seconds pause)
68. Your health is most important for you (7 seconds pause)
69. You breathe fresh and clean air (7 seconds pause)
70. Your lungs are getting healed (7 seconds pause)
71. Your body is your sacred place (7 seconds pause)
72. You love yourself (7 seconds pause)

73. You are full of vitality and energy (7 seconds pause)
74. You love to exercise because it makes you happy (7 seconds pause)
75. You are releasing weight effortlessly (7 seconds pause)
76. You are willing to change (7 seconds pause)
77. You let go of the past easily (7 seconds pause)
78. You are getting energetic with every passing day (7 seconds pause)
79. You pay attention to your sleep (7 seconds pause)
80. I am strong and healthy. (7 seconds pause)
81. You drink at least eight glasses of water everyday (7 seconds pause)
82. You look forward to your daily workout sessions. (7 seconds pause)
83. You listen to the signal and stop when you have eaten enough (7 seconds pause)
84. You are healthy and happy (7 seconds pause)
85. You love to exercise everyday (7 seconds pause)
86. You love to eat fruits and vegetables everyday (7 seconds pause)
87. You are becoming stronger and slimmer with every passing day (7 seconds pause)
88. When you crave sugar, you eat natural foods (7 seconds pause)
89. You are grateful for your health (7 seconds pause)
90. You are practice gratitude everyday (7 seconds pause)
91. You are open to new ways of eating (7 seconds pause)

92. You choose food that make your body stronger and healthier (7 seconds pause)
93. You chew food slowly (7 seconds pause)
94. You relish each mouthful and chew food at least 10 times (7 seconds pause)
95. You are becoming slimmer and lighter every day (7 seconds pause)
96. You love your body and mind (7 seconds pause)
97. You enjoy taking care of your body and mind (7 seconds pause)
98. You maintain sleep hygiene everyday (7 seconds pause)
99. You limit your day time naps to 30 minutes (7 seconds pause)
100. You can do it (7 seconds pause)
101. You are flexible (7 seconds pause)
102. You listen to your body (7 seconds pause)
103. You eat in moderation (7 seconds pause)
104. You eat wholesome foods (7 seconds pause)
105. You leave your past behind (7 seconds pause)
106. You feel decisive and enthusiastic (7 seconds pause)
107. You love your life (7 seconds pause)
108. You set everyday sleep and weight loss goals (7 seconds pause)
109. You take everyday actions to achieve goals (7 seconds pause)
110. You are motivated (7 seconds pause)
111. You focus on the good (7 seconds pause)
112. You are grateful (7 seconds pause)
113. You are happy (7 seconds pause)
114. You are self-aware (7 seconds pause)
115. pause)
116. .You see beauty in your body (7 seconds pause)
117. You learn new ways easily (7 seconds pause)
118. Your body is getting healed (7 seconds pause)
119. Every day you wake up you have feelings of gratitude (7 seconds pause)
120. You trust the process of life (7 seconds pause)
121. You trust yourself and trust your body (7 seconds pause)
122. You love yourself (7 seconds pause)
123. You are compassionate towards yourself (7 seconds pause)
124. You eat mindfully and enjoy every mouthful (7 seconds pause)
125. You are balanced (7 seconds pause)
126. You are competent and capable. (7 seconds pause)
127. You are worthy of love and care (7 seconds pause)
128. You give all the love and care to your own body first (7 seconds pause)
129. You choose positive thoughts (7 seconds pause)
130. You are blessed and abundant (7 seconds pause)
131. You love yourself unconditionally (7 seconds pause)
132. You are complete and whole. (7 seconds pause)
133. You are confident and courageous (7 seconds pause)
134. You forgive yourself for all the past mistakes (7 seconds pause)
135. You stay in present and are more mindful (7 seconds pause)
136. You are confident (7 seconds pause)
137. You have high self-esteem (7 seconds pause)
138. You are losing weight every day (7 seconds pause)
139. You are focused on your weight loss journey (7 seconds pause)
140. You pay attention to your food intake (7 seconds pause)

141. You love yourself unconditionally (7 seconds pause)
142. You are successful (7 seconds pause)
143. You are confident and motivated (7 seconds pause)
144. You believe in yourself (7 seconds pause)
145. You are good enough (7 seconds pause)
146. You enjoy healthy foods (7 seconds pause)
147. You do pleasurable activities everyday (7 seconds pause)
148. You are intelligent and wise (7 seconds pause)
149. You are lovable, open to receive and give love (7 seconds pause)
150. You enjoy your life (7 seconds pause)
151. You enjoy healthy food (7 seconds pause)
152. You have a beautiful relationship with food and your body (7 seconds pause)
153. You enjoy sleep and able to relax yourself easily (7 seconds pause)
154. You enjoy the process of self-hypnosis (7 seconds pause)
155. You enjoy being successful (7 seconds pause)
156. You inspire people by overcoming smoking (7 seconds pause)
157. You enjoy the benefits of being a non-smoker (7 seconds pause)
158. You imagine living a wonderful and long life as a non -smoker (7 seconds pause)
159. You spend more time with your family (7 seconds pause)
160. You let go of all the unhealthy habits (7 seconds pause)
161. You are success (7 seconds pause)
162. You are love (7 seconds pause)
163. You are happy (7 seconds pause)
164. You are positive (7 seconds pause)
165. You have high self-worth (7 seconds pause)
166. You enjoy living a quality life (7 seconds pause)
167. Life is wonderful (7 seconds pause)
168. You enjoy each day and live it to the fullest (7 seconds pause)
169. You are productive (7 seconds pause)
170. You enjoy being a non smoker (7 seconds pause)
171. You are a non smoker (7 seconds pause)
172. You are living a smoke free life (7 seconds pause)
173. You hate the thought of smoking and cigarettes (7 seconds pause)
174. You enjoy every day (7 seconds pause)
175. You are a healthy non smoker (7 seconds pause)
176. You are healthy and enjoy being healthy (7 seconds pause)
177. You keep your health on priority (7 seconds pause)
178. You enjoy all the benefits you see as a non smoker(7 seconds pause)
179. You are loved (7 seconds pause) (7 seconds pause)
180. You are open to give and receive love (7 seconds pause)
181. You are in control (7 seconds pause)
182. You have high control on your habits and thoughts (7 seconds pause)
183. Your health is getting better with every passing day (7 seconds pause)
184. Your body is healing (7 seconds pause)
185. Your body is getting repaired from the smoke (7 seconds pause)
186. You lungs are healing (7 seconds pause)
187. You protect your inner child always (7 seconds pause)
188. You are whole and complete (7 seconds pause)
189. You love yourself unconditionally (7 seconds pause)

190. You are a non-smoker (7 seconds pause)
191. You take care of your health always (7 seconds pause)
192. You exercise regularly (7 seconds pause)
193. You eat healthy foods (7 seconds pause)
194. You enjoy the tastes of healthy foods (7 seconds pause)
195. Your sense of taste and smell is getting better with every passing day (7 seconds pause)
196. You listen to this recording regularly (7 seconds pause)
197. You are a healthy non-smoker (7 seconds pause)
198. You are assertive (7 seconds pause)
199. You easily say NO to cigarettes (7 seconds pause)
200. You are an example for smoking cessation (7 seconds pause)

Quit Alcohol Hypnosis: Beginners Guided Self-Hypnosis & Meditations For Overcoming Alcoholism, Alcohol Anxiety, Increase Confidence, Rapid Weight Loss & Improved Health+ Deep Sleep

By Meditation Made Effortless

Copyright © 2020

All rights reserved.
No material in this book is to be utilized, reproduced in any electronic form, including recording, photocopying without permission from the author.

Table of Contents

Introduction 1

Induction 2

Deepener 4

Script for Attaining Deep Relaxation 5

Script for Healing the Inner Child 7

Script for Strengthening the Immune System 10

Script for Strengthening Motivation 12

Script for Overcoming the Compulsions 14

Script to Strengthen the Ego 17

Script for Good Health 20

Deep Cell Healing 22

Confidence and Self Esteem Script 25

Letting go of Alcohol Visualization 29

Alcohol Cessation I 33

Binge Drinking 36

Social Drinking 39

Alcohol Cessation ii 42

Alcohol Session III 44

Alcohol Session IV 46

Alcohol Session V 48

Healing the Past 55

Exploring Coping Strategies 60

Sleep Better 62

Affirmations 65

To the Narrator

The Introduction, Induction, and Deepener should be 45 Min Long
Deep Relaxation should be 20 min long
Healing the Inner Child should be 10 Min Long
Strengthening the Immune System should be 15 min long
Strengthening the Motivation should be 20 min long
Overcoming the Compulsion should be 20 min long
Strengthening the EGO should be 15 min long
Good Health should be 25 min long
Deep Cell Healing should be 20 min long
Confidence and Self Esteem should be 15 min long
Letting go of alcohol Visualisation should be 15 min long
Alcohol Cessation I should be 15min long
Binge Drinking should be 15 min long
Social Drinking should be 40 min long
Alcohol Cessation II should be 20 min long
Alcohol Cessation III should be 22 min long
Alcohol Cessation IV should be 25 min long
Alcohol Cessation V should be 40 min long
Ways to Sobriety 15 min long
Exploring Coping Strategies should be 15 min long
Sleep Better should be 25 min long
Affirmations should be 90 Min long

"…" means take a breath while speaking before you continue.

PAUSE (for a few breaths)

LONGER PAUSE (give time to allow the listener time to imagine what you've suggested)

Introduction

Thank you for choosing **Alcohol Cessation** ...and choosing this audio only means, you have taken a step towards loving yourself even more.

You may have realised the cons of drinking and that is the reason you are listening to this audio. Well, congratulations on becoming aware and thinking of quitting alcohol to bring innumerable benefits to your health and relationships.

Alcohol in the past may have given you temporary pleasure but when taken in excessive quantities, it changes the chemical balance in the brain that leads to negative thoughts and emotions. It not only affects the chemicals in the brains but also directly affects the skin, pancreas, liver, and appetite.

There are many short term and long term side effects of consuming alcohol. Some of the short term effects of excessive or regular drinking are memory lapses, vision impairment, slurred speech, slowed breathing, and lack of coordination. In addition, it also affects the people around you, especially your partner and children, if you may have. It may also influence you during driving, which may result in accidents or unnecessary arguments.

You have chosen to overcome this old habit of yours, which is indeed a huge decision that will reap many benefits, in every area of your life.

This audio recording will not only reinforce the decision of quitting alcohol but also reprogram your mind to relax your mind, body, and sleep better. This will help you manage your stress better and will eliminate the craving of having a drink.

Pause

So, congratulations on taking this step of quitting alcohol for good and making a wonderful decision to better health.

Pause

I would like you to sit or lay comfortably, where you will not be distracted. Do not listen to this audio when your mind requires your conscious attention.

Pause

Listen to this audio only when you are relaxed and stationary. Please use headphones so that you can focus on the sound of my voice.

Let us start...

Begin recording

Induction

You are now listening to the sound of my voice... and the sound of my voice only ...and as you continue to listen to each word I say...you allow yourself to relax more and more.

Pause

I wonder if you could take a deep breath...hold it for a count of 5... and then exhale.

Pause

Let's start now.

Breathe in Deeply...

Pause

Hold for a count of 5

1... 2...3...4...and 5

Now, exhale...
Pause

Once more, take another deep breath...

Breathe in...

Hold for a count of 5 — 1, 2, 3, 4, 5 (slowly)

Now, breathe out...
Pause

Once more, take another deep breath —

Breathe in

Hold for a count of 5 — 1, 2, 3, 4, 5 (slowly)

Now, breathe out

Pause

And, come back to your normal breathing pattern...

Pause

— And, I wonder… if you could simply bring all your focus and attention to the centre of your eye-brows…with your eyes closed…try to look at the centre of your brows and focus on the point between them…that's right.

Pause

In a moment, I am going to talk to that part of you, which is highly creative…the part that knows exactly how to help you imagine or create anything with the help of your mind's eye.

Pause

And… I know you can do it… because everybody can…we all have a creative mind, that has the ability and capability to create and imagine images in our mind.

I know you must have imagined or visualized or day-dreamed many times in your life. And… our creative part helps us imagine and visualize. Isn't it?

With the help of our creative mind, we can visualize, imagine, write, paint, and dream…and I am going to be talking to that part of you today.

Pause

Deepener

Use the power of this part of your mind to visualize yourself standing at the top of a magnificent grand staircase. This staircase has ten steps that lead to a hallway. Take a moment to look around and notice the material this staircase is made of… touch the handrails and see if the material is iron, wood, stone, or something else… The more you take note of the sight and texture of this grand staircase, the more relaxed you feel.

In a few moments, I will begin counting from 10 down to 0 and at each count, you will take a step down this magnificent grand staircase… slowly and steadily… And at each step, you will begin to feel twice as relaxed and go twice as deep…

Beginning with your right foot first, take a step down at 10… soaking in the comforts of this deep relaxation…

9… allow your body to gently drift into this beautiful state of relaxation

8… going deeper and deeper into this blissfully relaxed state of mind

7… observe this comfortable calmness settling in

6… going down further feeling more and more relaxed

5… you're halfway there

4… feel your mind and physical body relax twice as much

3… you're so close to the last step that you can see the hallway clearly

2… almost there, observe the relaxation sinking deeper and deeper

1… deeply at ease, twice as relaxed

0… you have now reached the bottom of the staircase

Longer Pause

Script for Attaining Deep Relaxation

And now, as you continue focusing on the sound of my voice and the sound of my voice only, begin to take a deep breath... Inhaling deeply and exhaling slowly and gently.

That's right.

Take another deep breath here... A gentle inhale filling up your lungs... followed by a slowly cleansing exhale.

And now as you begin to come back to a normal pace of breath... you will begin to notice all signs of tension drifting away from you and your body... The more you listen to the sound of my voice, the more at ease you become.

Continue this journey, going deeper and deeper into this beautiful state of relaxation.

Gently begin to tighten your right hand into a fist strongly as if each muscle is tensed here... and now, relax and let loose...

Pause

Repeat the same for the left hand...tightening the fist and gently loosening it... Allow both your hands to now rest loosely as if they were limp until they reach the full state of relaxation.

Now, bring all of your attention to your eyelids... Begin to squeeze them tightly and then in a moment let go of the tension in your eyelids to let them be loose and relaxed...

And now it is time to send a big wave of relaxation rolling across your entire body... beginning from the top of your head down to the tips of your toes... Let this wave bring relaxation to every nook and corner of your body.

Pause

It is time to send a second, bigger yet calmer wave of relaxation sweeping across your body from your head to your toe... Filling you up with the deepest relaxation as you continue focusing on the sound of my voice that will make you feel twice as relaxed with each passing moment...

They say the third time's a charm... Send a third wave of relaxation radiating across your body from the top of your head to the tip of your toes and see how utterly relaxed and loose all your muscles are.

Pause

There is no end to the levels of deep relaxation you can attain... As such, notice how this deep and heavy relaxation has filled up your toes, the soles of your feet, and your ankles... And how with each passing moment, this relaxation doubles in magnitude as it moves into the calves of your legs, the knees, the thighs, and the hips...

This incredible relaxation fills up your waist, your lower back, your torso, and your chest... getting magnified at each part of your body... as it continues making its way through your shoulders, your neck, the back of your neck, and your face… loosening every muscle, making you feel oh so deeply relaxed…

Feel this incredible relaxation sinking into every muscle, fiber, and bone of your body as it makes its way to your eyes, your forehead, and the top of your head… You feel so deeply relaxed as your physical body loosens and relaxes…

Pause

There is so much scope to relax even further… And now, as I begin to count down from 3 down to 1, with each count allow yourself to drift even deeper.

Beginning at 3… You can sense this relaxation everywhere in your body…

2… feel your body drifting deeper becoming even more relaxed…

1… drifting even deeper

As you continue to focus on the sound of my voice that is guiding you into this beautiful state of relaxation you feel more and more relaxed the deeper you go… and the deeper you go the more relaxed you become.

You find yourself becoming a part of a loop of relaxation, calmness, and comfort… And all you can feel within yourself are blissful feelings… As I begin counting down from 3 to 1 once again, you will find this relaxation getting magnified even further…

Pause

Starting at 3… Feeling twice as relaxed

2… drifting deeper and deeper

1… feeling more and more deeply relaxed…

As your body relaxes, your mind relaxes… And as your mind relaxes, your body relaxes even further.

You can use this method of attaining such a deep state of relaxation each time you find yourself craving any alcoholic drink.

Pause

Remember that it's a matter of diverting your thoughts from taking an alcoholic drink to indulging in productive, growth-oriented activities… And with the help of such a diversion, you will be able to attain relaxation of the mind while the thoughts of alcohol fade away.

You will have better control over your thoughts… And better control over your thoughts would mean better control over the actions that follow those thoughts.

Script for Healing the Inner Child

As you continue to vest your attention in the sound of my voice, you will slowly find yourself drifting into an incredibly beautiful state of relaxation… The more focused you are to the sound of my voice, the more serious and steadfast your resolve to quit consuming alcohol and lead a healthier and happier life becomes.

Now, upon your next inhale, you will find yourself going back in time to revisit the first time you picked up an alcoholic drink.

Pause

You can do it just like everyone else… You are going back in time to the very first time you picked up an alcoholic drink and sipped it… And as I count you down from 10 down to 0 you will find your way deeper and deeper into the subconscious mind until you arrive at the first time you sipped an alcoholic drink…

Beginning at 10…

Drifting further down into the mind at 9…

At 8 it starts to become easier to find your way across your mind…

At 7 you find yourself going even deeper...

At 6 going further deep into your subconscious mind…

At 5 you're halfway there…

At 4 you begin to see a slightly hazy picture of the memory of the first time you picked up an alcoholic drink

At 3 the haze begins to lift and the scene becomes clearer and clearer

At 2 you continue moving deeper and deeper into your subconscious mind

At 1 you are almost there and you can see the scene with more clarity

And at 0 you have reached this memory

Pause 10 seconds

And now as you begin to explore the memory of the first time you picked up an alcoholic drink, begin to zoom into this scene in your mind and explore everything and everyone around…

Was it someone else who asked you to try it or did you decide to sip alcohol all by yourself?

Just bring your attention to the reason that made you pick up the drink before moving further back in time to when you didn't consume any alcohol at all… When you were happy and stress-free…

Going further back to an even younger age… yes, just like that.

Long Pause

Maybe you are very young at this time... Look around and explore this scene... How old are you? Where are you? What are you doing?

Take an even closer look at this younger self of yours... Pay attention to the clothes you are wearing, the hair, the skin...

This younger self is your inner child... Would you love him or her just like your own child if you had one? I am sure you will... As a parent, you would give all your love to him or her unconditionally... Isn't it so?

Pause

Today is an opportunity for you to meet this child... To talk to them... Spend some time with them... To tell them how much you love them, how much they mean to you, how much you want to protect them and keep them safe and guide them at all times...

And at this moment here, you already know how wiser you are by looking at how far you've come in all these years and all that you have gone through... And with the help of all that knowledge, you will be able to guide your inner child on how to navigate through life while giving them all your wholehearted support...

Advise your inner child and motivate them with the pearls of wisdom you have...

And side by side it is time to travel forward in time together to when this younger self grows older and is about to pick up the first alcoholic drink...

Long Pause

And now you have both arrived at the time when your past self is about to pick up an alcoholic drink... Because this is a situation you have already been through before and know the ill consequences of consuming alcohol, I would like you to talk to your inner child who has accompanied you about the damaging aspects of alcohol consumption, especially on your health...

Recall here how you have promised to nurture, guide, and protect your younger self...

Keeping this in mind, what would you like to tell your past self as they are about to pick up an alcoholic drink? I would like you to share a dialogue with him or her... Tell them about the effects you have experienced when you consume alcohol... What were the ill effects of such consumption that you went through... How many times did you try to quit alcohol and how many times did you relapse? Have a heart to heart realistic conversation here...

Pause 15 seconds

Stop your past self from picking up the alcoholic drink... Stop them here because this means they will remain free of alcohol consumption all their life...

Now it's time to once again move forward in time with your younger self and arrive at present... Take a moment here to congratulate and praise your past self for listening to you...

You and your past self are a part of each other… They exist within you and you exist within them… And at this moment right here, you are together… And it is now time for your past self to integrate with you and for both of you to become one complete entity… An entity who does not consume any alcohol and stays in the pink of health for the rest of your life…

Use the power of your creative mind to imagine and visualize this integration… The two of you uniting into one… As this happens, your resolve to not consume alcohol and become healthier, joyous, and confident gets strengthened ten times over…

In unison as one entity, you are going to lead an alcohol-free, joyful, and healthy life.

That's right.

Script for Strengthening the Immune System

As you enjoy this state of deep relaxation, you allow the recording to help your inner mind in guiding your immune system to perform to the fullest. It restores your body to a vibrant state of well-being.

Pause

It is not important for us to understand and remember the functioning of the immune system to know its normal operation. We should just understand that the immune system is a product of thousands of evolutions that knows how to function normally. The conscious mind's only task is to bring the immune system back to its normal functioning.

Pause

Imagine an image of a control room in your brain that has a number of dials, switches, buttons and levers, even though there is nothing of that sort physically present in your body.

Take a look at it now.

Pause

As you look at the control room, you see a large computer in the center of the room which is the master controller of the immune system.

As you look at the screen, you notice quadrants being illustrated on it that tell you the mistakes the immune system can make. One of the quadrants is shining red to indicate that the immune system is either over-reacting or under-reacting. You will also notice a black dot in the shining quadrant that indicates how much the immune system is out of balance.

Pause

You notice a button on the keyboard that switches off the autopilot mode of the immune system, and you to switch off the autopilot mode now. Now your immune system is finding balance automatically and is normalising and returning to harmony with all the wisdom built in through evolution the endocrine glands are controlled by a set of levers next to the immune system computer.

Pause

As the immune system was out of balance, the endocrine glands have also lost their balance. Starting with the pineal gland, you move the lever up and down to bring it to the centre position which tends the pineal gland to produce some normal hormones. As the pineal gland secretes normal hormones, imagine the gland producing some golden drops that are flowing through the body and making every part of the body harmonious and healthy. As you scan the control room, if you notice any red flashing signals, they indicate that some part of the body is not functioning properly.

Pause

You set the controllers of these body parts that are not functioning properly to the centre position so that they start functioning normally. As you set the controllers correctly, the red lights go off and green lights turn on indicating the proper functioning of the body. And now, you command your subconscious mind to automate all the positive changes that you have made today, and you switch on the autopilot mode back. gland by gland you set the controllers of all the glands right.

Pause

The pituitary gland, thyroid gland, the liver, adrenal gland, all are now producing healthy hormones and enzymes that make the functioning of your body normal. And as you set the controller of the endocrine gland back to normal, all the functions of the body become natural and normal.

Pause

Now you set your powerful inner mind to go where it needs to go to magnify each and every positive idea a hundred times over to accelerate the healing a hundred times better. Every time you take a relaxation break or listen to this recording, your mind magnifies and allows the immune system to work normally and properly. It is ideal to take a relaxation break at least once daily for 25 to 30 minutes.

Pause

Every time you meditate, pray, or relax, your immune system rejuvenates. As by taking relaxation breaks and meditating, your immune system works properly you feel emotionally, physically, and mentally stable and healthier.

Now ask your conscious mind to think about nature, or something that makes you feel comfortable and relaxed.

Script for Strengthening Motivation

By having lived and experienced the awesome life free from alcohol, you feel that you are now more motivated than ever... You feel upbeat and want to live this life every day... Each day feeling even better than the day before... Feeling healthier... Like the best version of yourself... You notice how you are glowing with the abundance of energy and vitality... Feeling incredible about yourself.

Walking along the road of the triumph of being free from all alcohol consumption, try and sense this new self of yours... How does it feel to have come so long past the critical crossroads of your life...

I want you to imagine your future self... A successful and sober you... feeling so proud of yourself... Praising yourself for your consistency and sincerity.

Pause

This road that you're one... This road of triumph... Look around and notice how beautiful it is... Look at all the lovely flowers waving the in the breeze and the lush green moist grass... The clear blue skies and the fresh air.

Bring your attention to the wonders of an alcohol-free life... Notice how confident and strong you've become as you continue feeling great about yourself.

Think about all the money you have saved by not consuming any alcohol... There is so much you can do with all that money... Perhaps buy yourself a new outfit... Or something to decorate your house... Maybe save up for a long due holiday... The possibilities are endless because of all the money you have saved day in and day out... These cumulative savings have opened so many options for you...

Pause

It is immaterial what you decide to do with all this money because you deserve to treat yourself with something special just for yourself... because you are so special... Notice how proud of yourself you are.

Long Pause

Look at the amazing human being you have become... You are dependable as you keep your word... You are diligent and consistent... You meant what you said when you quit alcohol entirely... And look how you've stood by it stoically.

Look at how far you have come... I wonder if you can go back for a moment to the time when you were still consuming alcohol... Imagine all the toxic people who surrounded you... Perhaps a friend who offers you a drink...

Pause

You can see how they are proceeding towards you with a bottle or can full of alcohol... How they are undoing the cap or cork and tilting the bottle or can in your direction...

And as this scene unravels… You begin to realize more and more how this person is not a friend at all… because a real friend helps you steer away from temptations instead of throwing them at you… A real friend helps you stick to your goals and stay determined to abstain from alcohol.

Pause

Can you hear yourself saying "No" to alcohol and mean it? Can you realize the power of your body and your mind discarding the alcohol? Now that you are aware of how alcohol is nothing but poison to your system… You don't want it… And as a result, you won't have it.

Long Pause

The moment you say "No" to alcohol, something incredible happens… You begin to experience this wonderful feeling of confidence, strength, and pride flowing through you… Filling you with an awesome sense of achievement.

Notice how fresh and strong you feel as you say "No" to alcohol and mean it… You outright deny the offer because you no longer consume alcohol now… And that is exactly how you want to be.

Every single day you feel lighter, healthier, and more joyful… You are full of confidence… You feel so much better because you no longer take alcohol…

Pause

And this feeling gets stronger… Your determination and motivation are strengthened… This makes you feel happier, fitter, and so much better than ever before…

And now that you are sober, you prefer to stay this way forever because this is so important for you… And with each passing day, all these suggestions are going to grow stronger, becoming more and more profound and powerful.

Script for Overcoming the Compulsions

As you continue to focus on the sound of my voice and the sound of my voice only, you begin to go deeper and deeper into a beautifully relaxed state of mind where you become more and more attentive to everything I say.

The more you relax, the prouder you feel about making such a positive change in your life… This change is going to bring so much confidence and great health into your life to make it all the more fulfilling.

With each word I say, you begin to feel more strongly resolute to welcome health and discard alcohol… Each time you listen to this audio, you will find your determination to stay off alcohol becoming a 1000 times stronger… You find reprieve from this gross habit… Each molecule of your being enjoys being healthy and more functional.

Pause

Your liver, your heart, your kidneys, your brain… Every single organ within you is thanking you for having made such an important decision.

You have so much more control over your choices… You feel proud and celebratory for making this decision.

There is a part of you perhaps who thought of having a drink… And there's a part of you who wants to live a healthy, alcohol-free life.

Pause

This part of you that wants to stay healthy is the part that you have become the closest of friends with… This part of you helps keep your focus on the lifelong goal of abstaining from alcohol consumption always… You are not going to give in to any temptations to become slaves of the same old habit ever again… Notice how incredibly wonderful it feels to be free and in charge.

You have complete control over your behaviours and your decisions… You have chosen this healthier, longer, and more joyous life that entails more awareness and alertness, fitness, strength, healthy mind, body, and soul, fresher breath, toxin-free body… There is no stench of alcohol in your breath and no drowsiness in your eyes.

With a fresher breath and a radiant appearance, you are more attractive to your friends, your partner, and your family.

Pause

Notice how coherent and well-balanced your thoughts are… How cleaner your mouth is… How stable your body movements are… How lighter your head is… How healthy your gut and liver is…

You are free from alcohol in every way… You have a healthier and happier life… You are sober for the entirety of your long and healthy life… No amount of stress or temptation can make you consume any alcohol anymore… You have healthier ways to cope with stress which keeps your body and mind free from harm.

When you stood at the end of two diverged paths, you could see one that led to the path of a non-alcoholic, stress-free, healthier, and happier life… You also saw the other path leading to alcohol consumption and all its ill-effects.

Pause

And every bit of your being came together to help you walk the alcohol-free path… The path that you have taken and will always take is the one that leads to a happier and healthier life, free from alcohol…

Pause

Every time you encounter the slightest thought of alcohol, you reject it outright… You are reminded of the path that you have chosen, an alcohol-free life… It reinforces that you have made this choice and you are responsible for walking on it… This fills you with more confidence, making you feel more determined to bring about positive changes to your life.

Pause

If you happen to be around any alcoholics, you feel like you have never had a drink at all… And the stench of alcohol in the air that prompts you to reject alcohol is 1000 times stronger… You are filled with a sense of pride and confidence each time you reject an alcoholic beverage or even the thought of it… You gain more and more respect for yourself which in turn makes you feel more courageous.

Pause

You are also reminded of all the money you have wasted in the past on alcohol… And how you can save more money now with this impeccable decision… Perhaps put that money to good use… Investing it in better and more productive experiences or things… Perhaps to learn something new, to improve your fitness with a gym membership, maybe save up for a big holiday… There are endless possibilities.

Pause

All this, because you have made the choice to abstain from alcohol consumption and that is the new truth of your life which is embedded in the deepest part of your being to guide you as you navigate this brand new life as a non-alcoholic.

Long Pause

The truth remains that you are a non-alcoholic… You keep hearing your mind say it to you every now and then… You may hear, "I love being free from alcohol", "I am sober for life", "I choose to be sober", "I reject alcohol", "I think and feel sober"… Though iterations may vary, the meaning remains the same…

This new truth is safely locked into the depths of your subconscious mind… This makes it your reality as you continue living in this world with this truth.

Pause

Another new truth is, "I have NO desire to consume alcohol. I completely reject alcohol consciously and subconsciously."

And this truth too goes further down into the deepest part of your mind and becomes your new reality.

Another truth is that alcohol is a thing of the past... You have left alcohol way behind in an inaccessible part of your past which holds all the ill-effects of alcohol... In the here and now, you are sober.

Pause

The truth now is, "I have moved on from my past. Alcohol is a thing of the past."

The next truth is, "I am a non-alcoholic. I am forever free from alcohol consumption."

And as these truths sink deeper into the depths of your subconscious mind, you feel confident, wise, and empowered.

Pause

You are a non-alcoholic... You have no desire to consume any alcohol... Alcohol is a thing of the past... You are free from the consumption of alcohol... You are absolutely in love and awe of your healthy body.

These new truths have locked themselves in your subconscious mind... You hear them echoing at the back of your mind like a melodious symphony... Each time you hear this truth, your determination grows stronger and more profound... Your resolution becomes unshakeable... This is your new reality... You choose to stay sober for life... Continuing to live happily and healthily.

As I begin counting from 5 down to 1, these truths will sink further deep into your subconscious mind.

Pause

Script to Strengthen the Ego

As you proceed to focus your attention on the sound of my voice, you begin to allow yourself to become more and more receptive as you go deeper into this relaxed state of mind.

You have made the resolve and you're completely ready to bring about important changes to your body… To make your life healthier and happier.

Pause

The more you listen to every word I say, the more aware you become of the times in the past when you felt proud and confident about yourself… Such a time could be in your teenage years or perhaps your adulthood…

Begin to recall that time now.

And as you call to mind those scenes and situations… I wonder if you can pick one such situation where you felt absolutely amazing, confident, happy, and had faith in your worth.

Long Pause

Now that you have chosen the said incident… It is time to watch it with your mind's eye… Start watching it from the very beginning where it started.

What did you do? How did it make you feel? What did you think about yourself?

As you become more aware of the answers to these questions as you watch this incident… Notice all the positive emotions rushing through you as you soak in the delight of this memory…

Long Pause

As you draw near the end of the incident, it is time to watch the same incident once more, but this time on a big television screen… Or an even bigger projector screen… In high definition… While you sit on a comfortable couch with the remote control in your hand…

I wonder if you can visualize this great incident playing on such a big screen… in all its glory… This incident which made you feel so amazing about yourself, so proud of yourself… So happy and confident about yourself.

As this incident starts to play, you increase the volume to full…

That's right.

As this incident continues to play on this big screen in high definition and full volume… You come to the exact moment which instilled in you the maximum confidence and joy.

And as this moment starts to play… You zoom in the scene ten times over to watch it closely in all its glory…

That's right.

Pause

You can use the remote control to make the colors more vivid in ultra-high definition.

This incident is now loud, crystal clear, and vividly defined.

I wonder if you can take a mental picture of this scene right here and store it for safekeeping somewhere in your mind.

Find a suitable place in your mind to store this picture.

Long Pause

I want you to know that you will always remember the location of this picture in your mind… And each time you begin to feel low, you can simply use this picture to remind yourself about all the courage, confidence, and joy that resides within you… You achieved it once, you can achieve it again… Use this picture as a source of empowerment.

Long Pause

I wonder if you can make it a habit of practicing to fill yourself up with this a special color of confidence each morning when you wake up… To have an amazing start to your day that sticks with you throughout.

Imagine what this color of confidence might be… A color that is special and resonates with you.

Pause

Now that you have your special color of confidence… Allow it to steadily fill you up… Moving into every nook and corner of your body… Filling up every cell, muscle, fiber, and bone.

Fill up every part of your being with this color of confidence… Which makes you feel joyful, positive, and full of energy.

With such confidence, high energy, and joy you can achieve your ideal goal weight… It becomes so much easier when you vest your faith in yourself and have high self-esteem and recognition of your self-worth.

Pause

You are well aware by now that you have been confident before… This makes you feel more confident now… And the more you practice filling yourself with this color of confidence each morning, the stronger your confidence will become.

This confidence helps you have a stronghold on your eating habits and lifestyle… It helps you lose weight by eating right and getting enough exercise regularly to burn off the extra calories.

With each passing day, your confidence grows in magnitude and strength… Your self-esteem and self-worth get magnified too… Making it easier for you to achieve your ideal goal weight.

You exude this confidence and it shows in your body language… The way you walk and the way you talk… Your friends and family are amazed to see this transformation.

Long Pause

Allow yourself to let go completely of all the fears, inhibitions, and negative emotions as they serve you no purpose… Allow yourself to feel only positive emotions like security, joy, satisfaction, confidence, and freedom.

Pause

You are well-balanced at all times… Always being mindful and living fully in the moment as you work to achieve your goals each day… Beautifully and constructively.

Long Pause

You stay cool and relaxed at all times… Focused and present… Feeling confident and secure.

Pause

Script for Good Health

I wonder if you can imagine being surrounded by a serene white light which is bright and warm… A light that is soothing and healing… You are completely safe in this light.

As you find comfort in this light, it begins to move into your body, filling it up slowly and steadily… Perhaps starting from the top of your head… Moving down towards your toes… Filling up every cell, muscle, fiber, and bone.

Pause

As this light fills your body slowly, imagine having small taps on your palms and the soles of your feet… Open these taps to allow all the negativity to flow out of your system… Creating more and more space for this white healing light to fill.

Imagine all the negativity to be like a thick, viscous, black substance… Feel the pressure it exerts as it oozes out of your system… Take note of the soothing sensation of the white light filling up the space it creates.

This dark viscous substance is made up of all your fears, sickness, and negativity… Feel the light pushing it all out of your system as it makes it way deeper and deeper down into your body.

Pause

As this light fills up every inch of your system moving from your head to your face, ears, neck, shoulders, chest, and arms… Filling you up slowly with warmth and positivity… Drawing out all the negativity and healing every cell, muscle, organ, and bone.

As this white light begins to slowly move further and further down your body, it continues to fill every inch your body with nourishment and energy.

Take note of how it heals your body as it makes its way down into your abdomen, waist, thighs, knees, calves, ankles, feet, and toes.

Allow yourself to accept this white, healing light more and more as it continues to fill every part of your being… It brings nourishment, protection, love, and care to every inch of your body inside-out.

Long pause

Pause for a moment here to do a quick, mindful body scan… See if there are any spots where this light may not have reached… See if there are any spots that still house that black viscous negativity… If there are such spots, know that it's okay… bring your focus and attention to these spots and send a blast of white light to expel every last bit of the negativity from your body.

Feel the white light driving out the black viscous negativity until there is nothing but this white healing light.

That's right.

Long Pause

Now that your body is full to the brim with this loving, healing nourishment and positive energy… It is time to close the taps you had opened earlier… Keep all this goodness intact as it gets magnified and concentrated within your body.

Take a moment here to soak in this new sense of joy and good health… Take in the feeling of what it's like to be free of all disease and discomfort.

Long Pause

From this moment on, sickness neither has a name nor a home… It is no longer a welcomed guest… It is no longer acceptable.

From this moment on, you are healthy, happy, and completely healed… You feel like a healthy person… You see yourself as a healthy person…

You have rid yourself completely of fear, sickness, negativity, and discomfort… You are loved, protected, and strong… You have reclaimed your mind, body, and soul.

From this moment on, you make positive decisions that aid the wellbeing of your mind, body, and soul… You live a healthy and fulfilling life… You attain a positive outlook in every aspect of your life to help you lead a long, healthy, and joyful life.

Deep Cell Healing

Now take a deep breath for 4, hold it for 2 seconds, and exhale slowly. . Just say "breathing in" as you are inhaling. While exhaling, say "breathing out." Repeat this cycle of breathing 6 times while you concentrate on your breathing.

That's right.

Breathe In…….Breathe Out

Another deep breath

Inhale deeply from your nose and ….exhale from your mouth.

Let's take another deep breath…

Deeply in from your nose…and out from your mouth

That's right…

Breathe in deeply…….and breathe out from your mouth now.

Take another deep breath….breathe in from your nose and breathe out from your mouth. Perfect.

Next, I want you to bring your attention on how your feet feel, and begin to picture a thick, white sand covering every aspect of your feet and toes, the bones of your feet, the joints in your ankles, between your toes, under the nails.

Pause

And as you begin to notice or visualise the white sand on and around your feet…I would like you to remove any discomfort that you may feel in your feet and toes, and let it soak in the sand. Make sure you get rid of every last bit of tension.

Pause

Whenever the feet are pain-free and totally comfortable, imagine opening the double doors at the bottom of the feet and let the sand float out slowly, taking all the discomfort with it.

Pause

Fill in the clean white sand in your lower legs, knees and thighs and feel the tension soaking into the sand as your legs become more comfortable and heavier. Open the doors beyond your knees and let the sand slowly drift out, bringing any tension with it.

Now push the sand up the mid-section of your body, engulfing your hips and buttocks. Our buttocks are the toughest muscles in our body and retain a great deal of tension so make sure that you spend some time here feeling each muscle fibre as it relaxes and lets go of stress and tightness.

Pause

When you feel heavy and deeply rooted to the ground in this place, imagining opening the gates on your hips and let the sand go.

Pause

With this cleaning sand, gently fill your lower back, stomach area, digestive organs, hands, lungs, ribs, arms, upper back and shoulders. Starting from your lower back, feel the relief of each vertebrae of your spine, stretch out to your shoulders and focus on dissolving any knots of tension that you might have in this region. Be sure that the sand dissolves any stress inside your bones that you can sense. Open your lower back gate, and let go of all the sand.

Pause

Relax and let go of any stress or tension your stomach area, feel any contaminants and stress that you may be holding in this region. Let go of any pain or tension. Little by little, you feel your chest becoming more and more relaxed.

Enable your back, lower jaw, face and head to fill up with the sand. Pay careful attention to the back of the neck where friction knots can be found, feel these melt away into the sand. That's right.

Pause

The head and the neck feel heavy; the shoulders relax and sink down. Feel the tension behind your head, and the sand go from the forehead. Then open the doors at the back of the head and let the sand drain away into the ground, and any stress you retained in this place. Now fill your body with a perfect, pure white light, from the tip of your toes to the top of your head. Your mind is now at peace.

Imagine this bright light bathing every cell in your feet; imagine it penetrating your cells, filling the cells with love and light.

Shift this energy up to your legs and let your cells fill up with this energizing healing and love. Picture each cell's structure getting stronger and stronger.

Emphasis on the knee cells and the hip joints. Feel the bright light infuse every cell, replacing any damaged cells. Note how big every cell is. See building up of the bone cells and restoring healthy bone tissue. Enable any stress to rise and break away in those places, flowing out of your body.

Pause

Run the soothing light up gradually to fill your body's trunk. Feel the light in your stomach, intestines, pancreas, kidneys, lungs, neck, ribs, spine, back muscles, and shoulder blades, soaking into every bone. Pay particular attention to any area that may be of interest to you.

Pause

Picture your spine's cells; see each cell sparkling with power and lustre. Feel your spine become stronger and stronger. Giving you all the support, love, and care.

With this energizing light fill up each of your nerve fibres. Take the stress out of your muscles and let it melt away. The nerves are good and work well.

Put the light up to fill your head, face and arms. Picture the cells getting stronger and stronger in this area; see how quickly the DNA structure repairs. See each of the cell multiplying healthily and perfectly. Your body is strong and good, and your cells are safe and powerful.

Repeat the following affirmations:

I am perfect (7 seconds pause)

My body's cells multiply healthily, in a healthy manner. (7 seconds pause)

My organs are solid, and stable. (7 seconds pause)

Every cell in my body is a perfect expression of safety. (7 seconds pause)
All the cells inside my body function in complete harmony with each other. (7 seconds pause)

Each cell inside my body works fine. (7 seconds pause)

Cells inside my body are quickly and rapidly repairing themselves. (7 seconds pause)

Each cell in my body is lovingly enclosed. My body is strong, fluid and full of energy. I have bones which are solid and stable. I love my body, and respect it. (7 seconds pause)

I listen to my body, and take care of its needs. (7 seconds pause)

I treat my body with the respect which it deserves. Let me relax and unwind my body. Cells in my body are multiplying well. (7 seconds pause)

Every day I give positive energy to every cell in my body. (7 seconds pause)

I am so thankful to my body cells for keeping me strong and safe. (7 seconds pause)

Please take a moment to feel gratitude and happiness for your wonderful life and the unceasing wonders it brings.

Confidence and Self Esteem Script

Your mind will enter a relaxed state of mind and you will become more receptive to my suggestions.

Pause

Your subconscious mind will become receptive to new changes, changes that can potentially change your life forever.

Pause

The aim is to provide you with a happier and productive life ahead. You will soon be free from the thoughts which were limiting you from being free.

Pause

Low self-esteem and low self-confidence have their roots mostly in childhood. The reasons vary from person to person. Maybe the person suffering from the above might have had a tough childhood or unfulfilled relationships.

Pause

The words said by people in childhood have somehow hurt the fragile and healthy emotional side of the human being and this has given birth to the deep-rooted issues. But the time has finally come to change the course of your life and your subconscious mind will do the work for you today.

Pause

It will scout for the old memories in your mind and filter out the unnecessary programs which have hurt you in the past. The aim is to erase those memories and give you a new perspective on life.

We all realize at some point in our life that we should have known what was about to happen to us at some point in the past and regret not knowing the consequences beforehand. It is impossible to know normally but hypnosis can reveal those unknown facts.

Pause

This is because in hypnosis, all our levels of our mind are activated and both the conscious and subconscious mind communicate seamlessly.

Pause

Without your realization, your subconscious mind is working on the background and filtering out the events which are regarded as obstacles. In simple words, the cleaning process or the removal of junk is going on in the background. All the misconceptions, false beliefs, and negative thoughts are pulled out from the deepest corners of your mind and thrown away. This is where the younger version of your mind is telling you what you could have known back then.

Pause

Your grown-up version is convincing the younger version of your mind with positive thoughts. Thoughts such as you never wanted to hurt anyone and only spread happiness and love among the people surrounding you.

Pause

The younger version is leaving no stones unturned to convince the grown-up version that you are talented and intelligent in your way and there is no place for doubts.

All your past doubts and fear you developed back in your childhood are now neutralized. Your negative thoughts are replaced with positive thoughts. Truth is the ultimate answer you were looking for and now you got it.

Pause

No matter what the others had to say about you, the truth can never be changed. You have evolved to be a new person with a fresh mind.

Now imagine you have become the younger version of yourself.

As a child, go back to the time when you were secure and safe with your thoughts. Now come back to the present phase. You will realize that it would have been nice if you knew already what you know now. Convince the child version that everything needs not to be bad and love is prevailing in life. Praise that child and bring out the happiness from within.

Pause

Now it is time to think about the facts you wish you knew back then. Tell your child version those things you know now and convince her to remember those facts always.

Repeat if required but convince her fully about the facts and make her accept them fully. All your past doubts are now replaced with new positive thoughts. The child will now grow up to be confident and a woman with high self-esteem.

When you are done convincing, just say in your mind 'I'm done'. The time taken to perform this act of convincing may vary from a minute to a few minutes.

Pause – 30 seconds

Wait for the response from the child and then proceed. Ask your child version how it feels now.

Remember that all the changes in the child version are the changes that are happening to you today.

These thoughts, the positive ones are channeling in and out of yourself and is modeling the child version at every level. As the child changes with time, you too change, because you both are the same entity. The child is your past, your present, and your future. By simply changing her, you can change yourself completely.

Pause

Finally, today you have made the child version feel better than ever. It has now become confident and has developed a good sense of self-esteem in himself. As a result, your present self feels confident and has developed great self-esteem. Thus, hypnosis has played its part in recovering you.

Pause

Your past self has been dwelling in the old and outdated programs. Outdated programs were full of negative emotions that needed to be removed for your good.

Pause

Your work and performance today were top-notch and now you deserve to rest. The subconscious mind needs to process new information to replace the old information.

Pause

Now you possess every ability which you needed to do whatever you want in this world. Speaking of intelligence, confidence, diligence, and emotional stability, you have it all now. Your gender, height, eye color, and hair color are perfect for you and you have everything to become successful in the future.

Pause

You have changed yourself to be the better version of yourself. You have grown stronger both physically and emotionally. Now you can create a new life full of happiness and success.

There is nothing that can hold you back now.

Pause

The old programs installed in your head were the root causes of your fear and delusion. All of those have now been removed and new programs have been installed.

Pause

You will now have a new perspective on life and you will see the good side of things from now on. Thanks to your subconscious mind, all the junk has been disposed of properly and now you are free from the bindings. You will be emerging out from hypnosis now and all the new information will be stored in your memory. This session has been a successful one and always remember that once you have gained wisdom, you can never lose it.

Pause

You have emerged to be a new self and all you need to do is explore yourself for more positivity and confidence along the way. You have become intelligent and the best version of yourself.

Letting go of Alcohol Visualization

As we know, concentration is the secret of strength.

As you maintain holding your consciousness on your breathing cycle, start to imagine yourself breathing in a shining, golden, bright light.

Pause

Create a picture that this bright, radiant light is filling up all parts and cells of your body. Now the energy of your body is climbing to a new level. You can feel the positive energy throughout the body.

Pause

You can feel the sensations through your fingertips as the golden light is escaping from it and the energy is wrapping itself around the body.

Immerse yourself in the bubble of golden, bright light. At present, you are on cloud floating in your golden bubble. Your body feels comfortable, warm, and sheltered in all manner of ways. You feel protected here from all the distractions.

Pause

As you continue to float in the golden bubble, more passionate, calm, and compose you become. Let us go back to concentrating on your breathing cycle, establish the same rhythm. Now with every inhalation say" I'm light, I'm love". Try to hold your breath for a few seconds and again while exhalation repeats" I'm light, I'm love.

Pause

Count till 1 to 4 and mention "I'm light" twice and I'm love" twice.
Hold your breath for 2 counts. Then exhale for the count of 4. Again say "I'm light" twice and "I'm love" twice.

Pause

Imagine yourself rolling in a deep state of peacefulness and relaxation. Everything around you is in silence, smooth and still. You are completely feeling enduring, carefree, relaxed.

Pause

Keep enjoying these minutes, of peace and internal quietness. When negative thoughts start arising in your mind, just let them go away and come back to the attention to your breath. Concentrate on your breathing cycle and a positive attitude.

Now as you maintain this breathing cycle, keep taking deep breaths, visualize yourself breathing in a positive, curing, light which is expanding in your lungs. Your lungs are expanding with this light, fill it with positivity. Inhale liveliness in your lungs. Stuff all your body with this bright light.

Pause

Let's go to a beer garden with your buddies. Imagine you are sitting there laughing, amusing, and entertaining yourself. You are completely enjoying the company of your friends. Two of your friends are Alcoholics in that group; they start drinking in front of you and offer you a drink.

Pause

Surprisingly, you will react by saying "NO Thank you, I don't drink anymore". Your friends will be stunned by your reaction and will congratulate you for the period you are off the alcohol. They will tell you the difference between your health now and then. Your health has improved a lot; you look like a new person.

Regardless you are away from the company who drink but you can somewhat smell the drink, and it concerns and attracts you. But you are so strong mentally, inclined, and motivated towards your goal that you will never think about drinking again. Your mind knows that it is not attracted to drinking. It is without the thoughts of drinking Alcohol.

Pause

While looking at your friend who is drinking you remember your days of old how your hair and clothes used to get a whiff. But now you are enjoying your surroundings, inhale the enjoyable smell of fruity, fresh smell of your shampoo. Smell the incense of your favorite perfume on your wrist and clothes.

Pause

Let us go back to your consciousness to your lungs. Keep breathing and concentrating now each time you are breathing visualize that you are inhaling heavenly, bright white light into your lungs. White color is the relieving color for your lungs. Now you are filling your liver with this positive white light. You can feel this light entering the tissues of your liver, fill it. While this light is permeable to the liver and each cell is becoming stronger and stronger.

Pause

At this moment in time, the white light is rotating in your lungs; it is not just giving positive vibes but also clearing away all the negativity and toxins.

Pause

Carry on with the breathing deeply, inhale the white light of positivity, and keep exhaling the toxins, stress, tension out of your body. Keep saying this to your mind "My liver is healing, my liver is healthy, my liver is healing, my liver is healthy. This determination will lead you to the aim of quitting drinking.

Pause

Now the scenario is that you can easily appreciate the condition of your liver when you were drinking and now when you have quit drinking. Your liver has started to change color, it is turning light pink, fleshy color. And you know pink is the color of healthy tissues.

Pause

Assume your liver as a baby, pale pink which is healthy, well built, and powerful. It can perform all its functions properly. The cells of your tissues are consistently renewing and restoring their cells to enhance its function as a baby liver you used to have.

Pause

Look at yourself you are a completely changed healthy person you wanted to be. Witness the transformation of your lungs how healthy and strong they are looking. Your lungs are well-pleased as they look pink and moist, they are healthy.

Now with such positive vibes in your mind encircle the liver, skin, and other organs with the golden, shiny light. This light will protect your body forever. It will act as a shield to protect you from all sides.

Pause

Repeat these suggestions after me:

I am entirely in charge of my life. (5 seconds pause)

I am self-controlled and have strong determination for my aim. (5 seconds pause)

As I am not an alcoholic anymore my body is at liberty to go back to its healthy state. (5 seconds pause)

I am not compulsive towards drinking anymore. (5 seconds pause)

My body is now healthier and fit as each day passes. (5 seconds pause)

I consider my body as a temple and I choose to respect it. (5 seconds pause)

I am confidently and peacefully surrendering the habit of drinking alcohol. (5 seconds pause)

With each day passing, I notice more constructive changes in my body. (5 seconds pause)

I can effortlessly take control of my habits. (5 seconds pause)

I have a right to be a non-alcoholic person. (5 seconds pause)

I am the chief of my mind and body. (5 seconds pause)

I breathe completely and deeply. (5 seconds pause)

I make the choice to live a healthy lifestyle. (5 seconds pause)

My desire for negative thoughts will pass comfortably. (5 seconds pause)

My blood is full of nutrition and can function properly. (5 seconds pause)

My liver and other organs are healthier than before. (5 seconds pause)

Pause

And now take a minute to acknowledge and appreciate your wonderful life and the phenomenal things that are happening to you.

Alcohol Cessation I

Now that you have total control over your life and you are much motivated, positive and better at taking crucial decisions in your life, things are so better around you!

Your control over your desires and reactions are totally under your control and even the wish for alcohol is controlled by you.

Pause

Alcohol acts as a support for the weak and you are sure that you aren't weak; rather you are upright and confident about yourself and have tremendous will power of the mind. Isn't it?

Pause

There is no one else than yourself that deserves your trust now and you always know that your subconscious mind won't let you down. It will instead guide you towards the right decision in your life and let you do the things which suit the situation to its best.

Pause

The positivity in you is further allowing you to cope with whatever problem that comes in your life. Due to such a drastic change in your attitude, now you have lesser problems in your life too! Your struggling relationships are slowly coming back on track and getting better.

Pause

Yes, you cannot deny it anymore but yes you are moving towards a positive change now and it is helping you to be more relaxed. Your choices are changing and it is making all the difference. The fresh taste of clean water now excites you can makes you feel healthier than before.

The taste of non-alcoholic beverages are being enjoyed by your taste buds and you relish the fact that you are in control- which you lacked some time back. The complete control over your mind and body makes you feel freedom, which is priceless.

Pause

You choose what you eat and drink now. You, with all the senses, choose to only put good and healthy things on your tongue and alcohol is a poison to your health. Be it your brain cells, feelings or your self-respect, alcohol kills it all. Do you really deserve that? No, you deserve greater things in life because you are a great personality and an upbeat human being who is irreplaceable. The feeling of loving yourself more and respecting your dignity is hence very special and dearer to you.

Pause

Do you remember those days when you hardly had any sense about time and date due to the consumption of alcohol? Your voice and body both slurred and you lost every bit of control. The next morning when you woke up, hardly remembering anything of the last night and with a dominating headache due to the hangover- What could you say or do? Did you have a response to these?

Pause

The luring effect of alcohol made you forget everything about your liver, kidneys, stomach and brain and you just couldn't wait to have your next glass of alcohol again.
The good news is that period is over now and you are in total control of yourself. You no longer want to drink alcohol. The simple fact that alcohol is not necessary for healthy living is registered in your mind and hence you are able to live without it.

Pause

Now, imagine yourself with your favourite alcoholic drink- whatever maybe your preference.

Pause

You take the bottle up and the glass body under your fingers feels hard. The bottle is heavier than it felt before and the smell of alcohol is suddenly a lot more unpleasant than it used to be.

Pause

You go straight to the sink and slowly empty the contents of the bottle into the sink with the running water of the tap. The deadly liquid flows out of your bottle and makes it way into the plug-hole and finally disappears. As soon as the alcohol is drained out totally, the desire of your body to have another glass of the fatal drink is surprisingly vanished too!

Pause

Alcohol is the poison your system craves for but your mind denies and hence you say a big NO to it from now. When you say a NO you stick to it, that's what gentlemen do!
Now you think of a struggling situation in your life when you would have turned to alcohol.

Pause

Feel this for real, note the place of your presence and the companion, sounds and if possible any smell that accompanies this situation.

You know that you can drink alcohol anytime, but it doesn't bother you anymore. It doesn't matter because you are totally free from any addictions or whatsoever. The negative thoughts and the urge to have alcohol is no more present.

Pause

Instead, there's a relaxing sense of confidence and serenity around you just because you have learnt to say NO to alcohol. The feeling of self-respect is worthy and you feel that you are gaining back your lost esteem. Believe that you are a good person to be wit5h and your mind is driven by your powerful will.

Binge Drinking

You currently feel truly good and relaxed - and your inner mind is prepared to acknowledge each suggestion that is presented to you and follow up on it. The suggestions will dive deep into your inward mind and have a prompt and enduring effect on you.

Pause

In addition, since you used to feel awkward drinking liquor, you are here today.

Pause

You have just settled on an awareness level that the time has come to stop drinking - and now we simply need your inner mind to acknowledge your choice.

Get in touch with your awareness and imagine that and the chief and their worker - the manager sits in the workplace throughout the day - orders the workforce to execute them - however a specific representative is not content with a part of their activity - and needs to accomplish something other than what's expected.

They truly attempted to take care of business - however were adjusted to carry out the responsibility a specific way.

Pause

In addition, in light of the fact that the specialists have characterized their job - this rolls out these improvements troublesome - as well as about outlandish - because the chief has not yet concurred.

Indeed - the supervisor doesn't have the foggiest idea about the worker isn't content with what the individual has - on the off chance that the person in question is it is certain they will tune in and give a valiant effort to comprehend.

The supervisor will like the worker and prize him for his drive - through a pay increment or some other advantage.

Pause

It appears as though there was an absence of correspondence between the two - that is the reason now - we will get endorsement from your inner mind - and we are very brave on the most proficient method to push ahead.

Therefore, you've chosen it's an ideal opportunity to connect with the chief - and you need to envision setting off to the workplace and thumping on the entryway.

In the event that it feels great to converse with your chief, you will be brought in.
In addition, when your inner mind is prepared – you will get a signal from your inner mind and you will make a note of it.

Sit tight for a sign.

That is acceptable - presently open the entryway and go in.

You will be approached to plunk down - make your solicitation.

You may quit drinking liquor now?

Pause

On the off chance, that your psyche mind concurs that it will react by imparting a sign to your correct finger - and you can permit that finger to lift. On the off chance, that it does not your inner mind brain will react by imparting a sign to the pointer on the left hand - and you can permit that finger to lift as a sign to me.

Pause

On the off chance that you get no reaction, at that point you should work through whatever obstruction your psyche needs to consent to. Talk about your customer's issue until you get a full understanding.

Pause

Much obliged to you - Now as an arbiter between your brains – it would be preferred to make a proposal on the most proficient method to encourage your new want to quit drinking.

If it is not too much trouble demonstrate yes if both your cognizant and oblivious personalities concur on this.

Pause

What if the psyche is considering helping (customer's name) disregards drinking liquor and exiles any hankering?

Pause

Sit tight for a yes signal - if the appropriate response is no, inquire as to whether it has a superior thought and work with it - expecting proceeded with acknowledgment as follows.

Pause

Much obliged to you subliminal for submitting and consenting to this.

Now, as is it tallied down from ten to one - you will twofold your unwinding score with each number that is being checked.

Ten - twofold this unwinding - nine - twofold unwinding again - eight - more profound, more profound and more profound - seven - six - continue multiplying this unwinding - five - twofold solace - four - loosen up twice - three - more profound still - two - and one.

You will see that starting now and into the foreseeable future you can disregard drinking alcohol - just overlook drinking it.

Have you at any point had the experience of going into a space for something and when you arrive - overlook what you went for?

This is actually, what it resembles now with drinking liquor - essentially neglect to drink it.
In addition, it's so natural to overlook - similarly as you neglected to put your shoes on now - to remind you.

Pause

On the off chance that the possibility of alcohol gets into your psyche - you will overlook it in a split second - and it is simple like A B C - to overlook - and accomplish something other than what's expected - have a ton of fun.

Furthermore, when you neglect to drink liquor - you find that you are compensated from multiple points of view - better wellbeing - more pride - additional cash - a lovely sentiment of certainty - sharpness and concentrate constantly - on the grounds that you are liberated from drinking limitations. A great deal!

Pause

Consistently you feel much improved, more advantageous, more joyful and more in charge.

You feel good - but then - in entrancing - you feel superbly loose and loose.

Social Drinking

You are currently profoundly feeling relaxed and are agreeable, and your mind is open and responsive to the suggestions you are going to hear.

Pause

You are tuning in to me today since you understand that you have been drinking more alcohol off late than you needed to - and now you need to make another, more advantageous example of essentially having an odd mixed beverage when you're in social situations.

So first, it is important to compliment you for settling on this choice - because it shows that you truly comprehend the risks of getting dependent on liquor.

Pause

It is certain that you understand – extreme consumption of alcohol is a toxic to your body - it can cause issues with your liver, kidneys, stomach, and heart.

Pause

Liquor can likewise influence your ordinary everyday life - particularly when individuals lose their inhibitions.

Pause

It can likewise influence social, work, and general personal satisfaction - and obviously - the principal thing alcohol hinders your reasoning and feeling of judgment - no big surprise it has frequently alluded to as Satan's beverage.

However, you are putting the entirety of this behind you, and starting now and into the foreseeable future you will restrict your liquor use so you generally fall inside the suggested rules.

Pause

You will likewise quit drinking alcohol at home - aside from where conceivable in specific circumstances - maybe in the event that you are inviting visitors or praising an exceptionally unique occasion.

In any case - you may find that you hate it a similar way you used to - and that is all right - on the grounds that you are more joyful when you are in finished control and your reasoning is sound.

The main thing you choose to do is to quit purchasing the containers, jars of wine, spirits, or lager - or some other mixed drink - and you will be wonderfully be shocked at the fact that it is so natural to do as such.

Envision the store or store where you go to purchase the liquor.

Pause

Perhaps you can see the store name on the whiteboard - simply take a cloth or eraser and wipe it off - the truth is out - simply wipe that store from your mind. When the board turns out to be clear so you can inhale a murmur of alleviation - as though that specific store does not exist anymore - and it does not exist anymore - at the forefront of your thoughts.

Pause

Since it is so natural to overlook the things we need to overlook - rather we recall why we decided to overlook them.

In the event that you ordinarily purchase alcohol nearby other markets - for instance a general store - at that point you need to envision this grocery store now. Recall his name and see the grocery store in your inner being.

Pause

At this point, you presumably know this store quite well - and in all probability you know its plan - where products of the soil are kept - where there are bread and cakes - the solidified nourishments segment and the various things that your general store sells.

Pause

At a certain point, you knew precisely where the wine, brew, spirits and other liquor path was found - however now you couldn't care less - so perhaps you can envision it simply isn't there any longer.

Pause

Furthermore, when you visit that store to do the shopping - you walk straight through the passageway - not in any event, seeing - you certainly couldn't care less - where it is - or not.

Pause

Furthermore, - on the off chance that you are having some good times or if there is an extraordinary occasion whereby you feel that you should serve liquor to your visitors - maybe you can approach another person to get it for you - on the grounds that you would truly lean toward not to go down this way.

Since you have quit purchasing liquor to drink at home, it will be a lot simpler for you to shed it.

In addition, obviously - you may have essentially become acclimated to drinking - for this situation how about we make a more significant elective propensity.

Also, there is a lot to look over - there is such a great amount to do.

You can gain proficiency with another aptitude, read your preferred books, paint, draw, or sew.

You can begin another leisure activity, fabricate models, become familiar with a language, and compose your biography or any number of fascinating things.

Pause

In the event that you for the most part drink alcohol late around evening time, you may now need to appreciate early evenings in bed - get a decent rest and rest or invest energy with your cherished one.

Pause

In addition, it's astounding how you locate that after only a couple of long periods of not drinking - the possibility of that appears to have vanished from your brain - you don't need it now - you needn't bother with it.

Indeed, even in social circumstances, you may find that you are not as distracted from the reality as you used to be with liquor.

Pause

You frequently lean toward a soda pop that you know is better for you and will last more.

Starting now and into the foreseeable future, liquor has lost its significance to you. You cannot envision what it probably been similar to when you drank at home - all you truly know is that you will be so glad to stop.

Pause

These proposals are immovably inserted in your mind and develop more grounded and more grounded step by step.

Get more grounded constantly, more grounded continuously, and more grounded constantly.

Alcohol Cessation ii

Individuals with liquor issues frequently need assistance with their confidence and some type of certainty building. Set aside some effort to discover what you are good at, and carry your benevolent sentiments into play with a physical reaction, for example, tightening your right hand fist. This will help direct consideration away from the inside reaction and engage you with the positive feelings.

Pause

"For quite a while now you have been acting and feeling in manners that separated you from your ordinary self. You have been increasingly dependent more on alcohol to assist you with defeating the negative emotions you have been encountering, and you have done as such to the point that you wind up denying yourself your actual feelings. Isn't it?

Pause

No one feels large and in charge constantly and there will be days that could be better for you. Just by encountering a portion of the lows in life, can you really appreciate and welcome the highs.

Eradicating your feelings with alcohol doesn't explain anything, it just exacerbates the situation, which is the reason you've chosen to listen to this audio. You have had enough liquor, and you truly need to help take care of your old issues.

Concentrate now on an aspect of your life that you feel cheerful in - you might need to recall something great that happened, something that caused you to feel certain, maybe an accomplishment or some amazing feeling of accomplishment or pride (Pause) ... presently notice how you feel inside, pride, certainty, and bliss - and let those nice feelings and thoughts to become more grounded, while you relax and let go.

Pause

Furthermore, when these positive emotions and feelings fill you, you need to take a full breath and tighten your right hand fist, while your inner mind safeguards those nice feelings and locks them in.

That's right.

Since when you like to feel as such, you should simply take a long full breath and tighten your right hand fist. Every time in future when you are stressed or feeling overwhelmed with the negative emotions, simply tighten your right hand fist.

Pause

Notice the feelings within you when think of having a drink and go to the bar or kitchen to grab a glass, you need to take a full breath through your nose and tighten your right hand fist while you recollect those positive, sure emotions.

Pause

You promptly feel better. It is a great idea to be certain and realize that you are liberated from the old, addictive lifestyle. Liberated from the weight of drinking alcohol, allowed to proceed with your awesome life, to encounter the highs, just as the lows, realizing this will push you to genuinely acknowledge when things improve.

Pause

You are evolving. Your perspective improves, your authority, you assume responsibility, you are in charge. You are completely liberated, liberated from the addictive way of life, and truly, there will be minutes where you feel torment, yet these minutes will diminish to an ever increasing extent, and you will truly value the pleasant things in life the easily overlooked details that cause you grin and to feel cheerful.

Alcohol Session III

Presently as you move further and into the profound relaxation ... more deeper, more relaxed…you notice all sounds blurring away and you just focus on the sound of my voice. Going further down and down, deeper and deeper. There are three stages to disposing of any alcohol issue. The initial step is relaxation and you are relaxing already.

Pause

Clearly, you must be relaxed and you are not totally relaxing in every way and in every shape or form right now, currently you need to totally unwind ... relinquish everything.

Let your arms and legs and your whole body completely go relax. Since you are relaxed than you were previously, the second point to quit alcohol is understanding the "why" of having alcohol. In addition, you completely comprehend it as a matter of first importance, in every occurrence of a drinking issue in your mind. The individual who tends to drink too much, including yourself, has been defined in your mind.

Pause

It could be someone in your family or your close friend who you relate to when you drink. Or maybe the reason is something else. If it is someone you know who has been a heavy drinker, then today is the day to simply cut the cords with that person. You do not need to be like him or her. You just need to be the real you. The one who wants to quit alcohol and is listening to this recording. This person is going to cut the cords with that person who perhaps introduced you to it or who you relate to more.

Pause

In a moment, in your imagination, I would like you to call that person and imagine a white cord being connected between the two of you. You notice the elastic white thick cord connecting you both and you notice it between the torsos.

Today is the day to let go of that person from your mind and spirit by cutting the cord. I would like you to imagine cutting the cord with a big garden shear. As you cut it, you notice the person leaves you and goes far and far away from you.

Pause (10 seconds)

That's right.

You are free from it. You are free from the energetic connection with that person from your life…who is a heavy drinker and you somehow relate to them.

Pause

The third stage is to remember the god or the higher power or the one you believe in. Just remember that and surrender. Surrender all your worries to him and you shall feel lighter and much more relaxed.

Everything will be taken care by the supreme power or whoever you believe in. Just trust the process of life and trust the one you believe in and you will be able to kick off this old habit.

Alcohol Session IV

You continue to drift into a deep relaxed state of mind, and as you drift deeper, you can hear my voice a lot clearer. You can see all other distractions slowly fading away. We are now going to help you get rid of all the suggestions in your mind.

Pause

And as you listen carefully, we will rid your mind from each and every negative suggestion now and forever. You are now completely focused on my voice and nothing can distract you in any way. You completely accept everything I say to you because everything I say is the absolute truth. We are going to rid your mind of every suggestion that has been detrimental to your well-being.

Pause

The first suggestion we are going to rid your mind of is alcohol. In the past you enjoyed drinking because you thought it made you feel better but now you know that the reality is far from it. You now know that alcohol is of no use to you . You do not need alcohol for any reason anymore. It doesn't help you relax and on the contrary it affects your sleep. Alcohol does you absolutely no good.

Pause

As a matter of fact, alcohol ruins your efficiency and since you have realised, you have now overcome the need for alcohol. And through this we have completely eradicated any suggestion of alcohol being beneficial to you. I am going to count to five and from that moment on, the suggestion that alcohol is beneficial to you will no longer exist in your mind.

One, two, three, four, five.

Pause

Let's move on to the next suggestion which is using alcohol to punish yourself. You no longer need alcohol to punish yourself because you have realised you don't need to punish yourself anymore. People only punish themselves because somewhere deep in their minds they feel guilty and you have now overcome this - you no longer allow yourself to feel guilty.

Pause

We are now going to empty your mind of all forms of guilt and along with that we will eliminate the need for you to punish yourself by consuming alcohol.

One, two, three, four, five.

And that suggestion has now been emptied from your mind. You now understand that alcohol is poisonous. It makes you sick and inefficient and so you have overcome the need to poison yourself.

One, two, three, four, five.

It's now time to rid your mind of all connections to alcohol. The only kind of alcohol you know or care about is rubbing alcohol. Rubbing Alcohol is wonderful, it's great to use for a nice back rub and that's the only use it has in your life.

Pause

You no longer associate alcohol as a beverage. The only alcohol you are aware of is Rubbing Alcohol and therefore we have rid your mind of all connections to alcohol as a beverage. You no longer think of alcohol as a beverage. You don't ask for it, you don't need it or desire it in any form. Even if you were offered alcohol, you would refuse it because you find alcohol disgusting. It tastes terrible and it makes you puke. Now, at the count of five, we are going to eradicate all negative suggestions from your mind and replace them with the new positive suggestion I have given you.

One, two, three, four, five.

From this moment on you are completely free from alcohol and it's entangling octopus like tentacles. You are free from it's self-punishing nature, free from it's clutches which was ruining your life. You are completely free because all the connections in your mind to alcohol have been emptied. We have unplugged the wires and it's not possible to ever restore it even if you would want to.

Imagine there's a huge telephone switchboard inside your head and all the wires connected to the socket marked "alcohol" are now removed and it won't work even if you try plugging it back in.

Pause

Alcohol disgusts you. You no longer want to buy it and even if someone offers you alcohol you decline because it has a foul taste. It has a terrible effect on you and makes you very uncomfortable to even think about it.

One, two, three, four, five.

Now you are completely free of the alcohol problem in every way. You are surprised and amazed by your self-discipline and confidence knowing that you have overcome your alcohol problem forever. Now sleep, sleep deeply and let your mind concentrate on the sound of my voice as you go deeper and deeper into a relaxed state of mind.

Alcohol Session V

Now, let me tell you how alcohol is poison for individuals with a drinking problem. It's poisonous in two ways.

Pause

Firstly, it's a psychological poison as it weakens your willpower, your ego and the faith in yourself. To give you an example, if you ever go back to drinking after overcoming the alcohol problem; you will notice negative thoughts & feelings returning to your mind. Thoughts such as "I'm good for nothing", "I really don't like myself" and so on.

Pause

Secondly, it's physical poison because you are now allergic to alcohol similar to how people have other allergies. And once you're allergic to something, even if it's something like penicillin, it's going to be poisonous to your system and you must never consume it. The same now applies to alcohol.

Pause

And so, since you are allergic to alcohol you no longer need it. Alcohol is poison to you.

Here's another interesting fact - people who are drawn to alcohol never really say good things about alcohol. You don't hear them say things like "It makes me feel good" or "I like the taste of it".

Pause

In fact, they speak of it in exactly the opposite manner. They say things like " I don't like it, it's terrible", "It's ruining my life". So why are they drawn to it even after knowing alcohol is not good for them? It's because in their subconscious mind they want to commit suicide, and so they use alcohol to punish themselves in a slow tortorous way.

Now that you understand this, you can see why it is so important to eradicate the underlying problem - that is the issue of punishing oneself.

Pause

We have therefore rid your mind of all the guilt, and since you are no longer guilty, there is no need to punish yourself anymore.

Let us leave that in the hands of the higher power.

From this moment on, you no longer need to punish or poison yourself. You realise alcohol is poison and you are therefore going to leave that poison alone. You don't need to punish or poison yourself anymore because you have rid yourself of such negative thoughts & suggestions.

You are now going to start appreciating yourself, you are going to appreciate the talents you have. You are going to acknowledge that you are special in your own way and you will appreciate the good life you have been given. You will now begin to see all the good deeds you can do in your life for yourself and for others.

Pause

There are certain terms that are synonymous with alcohol. Terms lie "He certainly got stiff" which is also used to describe a dead man. We also hear people use the term "Dead Drunk". It's interesting how the terms dead & drunk are often used together, isn't it?

Pause

It's because alcohol is poison, and you are now able to understand and see how alcohol is poison and therefore you are completely free and you no longer have the need for alcohol. In fact, you can't even smell it anymore.

Pause

You are just beginning to appreciate and value yourself. You are beginning to take good care of your mind and body. You are going to stay sober and by doing that you will make yourself and everyone else happy.

You will avoid alcohol like the plague. You will avoid it cause it's a substance that you are most allergic to.

Pause

And by avoiding alcohol, you have won a significant battle in your life and it's now forever placed behind you. You now have a beautiful future ahead of you and no matter what obstacle may come your way in the future, it will still be easier for you to face those challenges sober. You are going to be happier and have twice as much fun sober than you ever had when you used to be drunk.

Pause

Alcohol was only poisoning your system. It was killing you slowly but surely and it almost succeeded but you managed to rid your mind of all those thoughts and today you no longer see the need to punish yourself.

Pause

You are now going to start appreciating yourself and you are going to become stronger and be happier.

You no longer need to punish yourself. Now take a deep breath and with every breath you will feel yourself going into a deeper relaxed state of mind and all these new positive suggestions will be reinforced in your mind every single day of your life.

Way to Sobriety

You continue to drift deeper and deeper into a much more peaceful state and as you continue to do so, I wonder if you can imagine a big library somewhere. It could be a library that you want to create now in your mind or the library you have been before.

Pause (10 seconds)

That's right.

The library that you notice has many many books on many many shelves. And as you continue to look at the books on many shelves, you notice a shelf that has the books of your life.

Pause

That shelf has books from your life and each book has every little moment of your life that you have already lived. I wonder if you can take a closer look at the shelf with the books from your life now.

Pause

And as you take a closer look at the long shelf of books from your life, you notice that the right side of the shelf has all the inspiring and happy books. The books that have the positive moments of your life. You touch them and feel the texture of each of the book. You notice the colour and the cover page. Are they paper back or hard covered?

Notice..

Just get the knowing of each of the book as you continue to take a closer look at the right side of the shelf. Each of the books on the right side contains your goals, accomplishments, dreams, and good memories. These books have all the amazing things you have done in life and all the good things you plan to do in your life. All the positive emotions you have ever experienced with all the positive people. The right is the positive side.

Pause

The books on the right side also contains information about your talents and skills. This is the side of books that you are truly proud of you. You have achieved so much, you are amazing and good enough. It has the books from the times when you were appreciated, whether it was your school or home or work. Every book on the right side of the shelf has a positive story from your life. It also has books that describe your true nature and your personality. You are amazed at the collection of books and the information available inside.

Pause

The other side of the shelf, which is the left side has books that perhaps contain not so good memories from your life. Here, you will notice books that contain incidents and stories of the times, where you felt low, sad, angry, in the events you feel should not have really happened to you.

Pause

When you further look at the books on the left, you notice the shelf also has books about the various problems you faced in your life – whether emotional, financial, physical. All the books here are just opposite to the books on the right side of the shelf.

Pause

These are the books that sometimes hold you back in the past and do not do any good to you. These are the memories that serve no purpose and you sometimes seem to stay stuck in them, thinking about whys and hows of every situation.

Pause

Come to think of it, you have probably been reading just the negative books on the left and especially when you are drinking.

What do you get out of reading them? Sadness and negativity, isn't it?

Pause

It's been so many years that you have just been reading these negative books and you know there's no positive learning coming from them. They make you sad or perhaps angry. Whatever emotion you get when you read them, you know is is negative. Isn't it?

You have carried them along for too long. The time has come to discard them coz they do not add any value to you and your life.

You have decided to let go of all these books and decided to discard them in the trash can. Just outside the main door of the library, there is an extra-large trash can ready to take in all the old worn out negative books from the left side of the shelf.

Pause

You now go back to the shelf and take a carry basket to put in all the negative books holding every negative emotion and memory from your past that serve no purpose and make you feel sad.

Put them one by one in the carry basket.

Pause (10 seconds)

Now, take all those books to the big trash can and start dumping the books one by one into it.

Pause (10 seconds)

That's right.

And as you see the books in the trash can, you start to feel positivity encompassing you from all side. It feels as if the weight has been lifted up from your shoulders.

You go back to the shelf just to see if there are any more books that need to be discarded.

Pause

You take a closer look again and you notice that you have missed a few books that also contains your worries and stresses about future. And you know that you cannot let go of your present day thinking or worrying about the future.

And, there is no point in worrying, instead, you can plan and you can plan for the plan a and plan b so that you know that if something goes wrong, you know exactly what you need to do.

So, pick up those books and put them in the carry basket and dump them in the trash can, just outside the library.

Pause (10 seconds)

That's right.

Great job done! This is another step to loving yourself and knowing that you are full of love and give yourself all the care and attention. You have just gotten rid yourself of all the baggage that served no purpose.

You feel even more lighter now and as you were picking up the last set of books to discard, you noticed that there was a large hard covered book also lying on the shelf.

And, that got you curious and you perhaps thought that it's the book on the right, but it is lying just in the centre that divides the shelf in left and right.

You go back and pick that heavy book and open it to read the table of contents.

And, you notice that this books is about the problem behaviour, the book of alcoholism and this book contains everything you have done under the influence of alcohol, it may contain good memories but majorly it has bad memories.

You have decided to get rid of the book too so that you can only have a shelf of positive books in the library.

Take it in your hands and move towards the trash can. (Pause)

Move towards it with the book in your hand and simply throw it in the trash can.

You don't need it…at all.

Pause

You now go back to the shelf to check out the right side of the shelf. And, in those books, one book catch your attention that says : "My Book of Sobriety"

You take that book out and feel the texture of the book and smell it.

Pause

You decide to take a look at it and for that you look for a comfy chair to sit in the library. In a moment, you notice a comfy couch for you to sit and read the book.

You take a seat and rest in the chair and as you flip the pages, your conscious mind begin to drift away in the distance while the subconscious mind pays starts to pay attention to every word written in the book.

And as you begin to read, your subconscious mind opens itself to absorb the wisdom and knowledge. Whatever idea is written in the book, your subconscious mind happily and willingly accepts them.

Pause

You know that you are powerful to overcome any addiction or habit. You are much more powerful than your own thoughts and you can control them easily. You look forward to living a fulfilling and healthy life and you can achieve that by being sober. To have a thriving life, you embrace health and healthy foods and drinks. And, as you continue to eat and drink healthy, you begin to notice positive change in your sleeping and eating pattern. You begin to notice change in your environment.

I would like you to now embrace this beautiful and positive change and let your inner mind fill itself with the wisdom from the book.

I would be quite for a few moments.

Pause (25 seconds)

Now, come back to each word I say now. You are beginning to live a new life, a healthier and more successful life. You are a child of god and you believe in the process of life. You trust yourself, the god, and the process of life.

Pause

Now, simply continue to breathe and each breath you take strengthens each wisdom and word from the book. And the book says this beautiful prayer that you will embrace for the rest of your life and it goes like this:
Give me the serenity to accept the things I cannot change, the strength and courage to change the things I can, and the wisdom to know the difference.

With this, you look at the shelf of positive books from your life and feel positive and completely motivated to live a healthier and even better life from now on.

Healing the Past

You are relaxing your mind and taking deep breaths, with each soft, pleasant rhythmic breath, you are becoming calmer and relaxing more deeply. While breathing out, you are exhaling out all your stress, negativity, tension, discomfort. And during inhaling of each breath, you are inviting all the positive energy, calmness and peace into your mind and body.

Pause

You relax more deeply with each cycle of breath, your inner mind is much stronger and approachable to all the specific, beneficial ideas in this recording. With every single breath and beat of your heart, the mind is absorbing each positive suggestion for the purpose of healing. Your mind is absorbing these suggestions and building them as your inner and outer reality.

Pause

Your heart is having a beautiful place like a meadow, just like the place in the outer world. And the feelings are the same in the outer world or inner world. When you visit the inner meadow of heart, you are getting in a place of safety and flexibility. There you can be cheerful. It is always there for you. For visiting the meadow you don't have to listen to this recording really. It's a place where you don't require such things. All you have to do is just close your eyes, feel safe and you will be in the meadow.

Pause

As you are thinking about the meadow, a wave of stillness, calmness fills your mind. This feeling is not for a particular moment, beside it is deep and long-lasting regardless of what is happening around you.

Pause

You are now allowing your outer conscious mind to relax in the meadow and drift in the calmness and serenity. While the inner mind is doing all this work. The outer mind is listening to the instructions and following, the inner mind is the one that is doing the work.

That's right.

Pause

You may have experienced a lot of emotional pain and trauma in the past. The memories of that past are still with you and are present with you in your life. It is not only affecting physically but also mentally. All it is doing is just filling your current life with pain and fear, and inhibiting your choices in life.

While listening to this recording you are guiding your inner mind that the time has arrived to heal the pain you have been suffering. And its time you should live your life perfect and positively as you deserve.

When we experience a negative event, it causes emotional injury and if it causes tremendous pain than what we can handle at that time, it actually ruptures our mind.

Our mind is a great device if such issue is present it will keep that sensitive part in one corner of the mind and locks it so that we can grow and survive through it.

No doubt it is a constructive strategy that we can continue to live our lives with such immense pain that is so big to bear. Despite this, the pain is still inside us. That budding, sensitive part of the mind is still experiencing the same emotional pain, shame, anxiety, fright most of the times.

Pause

So the first step to healing for the mind and soul is to protect that younger budding part of the mind. You don't have to recall or look back to all those memories of past in detail even though you may remember some peculiar parts of it. But you don't have to worry as you are ready to cope up with it easily.

Pause

These memories are in your subconscious mind and that is why the healing will take place in your subconscious, underneath the surface. For the healing, all you have to know is that there is this small younger part of the mind that is still entrapped in old bad memories which are excruciating the pain in your present life.

Pause

Now imagine yourself as that child, it is not necessary that you have some remembrance of that time. You have to imagine your younger self in some kind of negative emotion.

Get the knowing of that negative emotion. It could be any emotion.

together with all your grownup strength get that child up and cradle the younger self with warmth and affection in your arms. And tell that child that " You are safe and protected now, no one can harm you... I am your future self. I am here to help you."

With the courage and stability deep-rooted in you have taken the younger self out from the old bad memories. You let him know that "You don't have to live that painful life ever again in future".

Pause

As you are strong enough it will be your decision to go back to those memories, but you don't have to live it again. And please notice the sign of happiness, satisfaction at the face of your younger self. Just by looking at the innocent face, you feel relaxed.

Now allow your younger self to move to the beautiful meadow of mind, the place of bliss and joy. Younger self will never face any pain in life again because you are always there ..the capable, wise adult. you are not only there to get through the challenges of life but you are there to blossom with every experience.

You convey the child the message that it has to explore the interest, pride, playfulness, cheerfulness of youth and return this contribution to the outer world.

Pause

At this moment you and your younger self are standing in the meadow, and you notice that sunset is going to happen. As you see the beautiful nightfall, you start to understand that this is the time when you will let all the injuries, the pain of the prior life into the past and make your upcoming life unbound to these bad memories.

Pause

With the sunset in your meadow, you are choosing a new path of life and letting these old issues disappear.

Imagine the Sun going down....and as it goes down, you let all the old emotional baggage disappear.

That's right.

You are completely enjoying the marvellous moment of sunset with all the ethnic group of colours orange, blue, red that are painting the sky. You notice the appealing light dancing in the clouds like waves and spraying all colours on you and your meadow. You are enthralled by the light and you feel this energy inside your life. By this energy, you can feel a sudden powerful upward movement and healing of the inner soul.

Pause

You grant the old memories to vanish from your life and become insignificant. these memories are just some old incident in the road of your life and they are fading into the past. And there is an old fashioned saying that "whatever doesn't kill us makes us stronger". By this time you can easily understand that you are a survivor and this has made you much strong, tough, buoyant, concerned human being. Till sunset, you are feeling more strengthened and refreshed.

You can witness your younger self relaxing, inclining towards the healing and regenerating sleep after so many years. The old soreness is dissolving away with sunset.

Pause

Straightaway I will ask you to do something challenging but the radiance of the moon in the meadow will make this challenge easy.

You have to forgive the individual or people who injured you emotionally.

Remember that forgiving someone doesn't mean that the incident never happened. It means that you will make a clear borderline so that it will not happen to you again. And if the person continues to harm you then you will take all emotional, communal, legal actions to stop them.

Pause

The main motive of forgiveness is that you will not have any bitterness, rage, uneasiness, vengeance in your heart for that person. It will not poison your heart.

Imagine the person who has hurt you is sitting on a chair, and he or she is listening to you. Then you will let them realize the pain, and details of how they hurt you and the consequences you are facing because of them. The damage they made was affecting your present.

Pause

Tell them your boundaries and that such wrong behaviour is never approved again. Let them listen to all your injury, pain and suffer. They should understand the pain they gave you not as vengeance, but directly so they realize what they did to you. PAUSE for 10 seconds.

Pause

Just give them a chance to reply. PAUSE 10 seconds..... Regardless whatever they reply or if they apologize, convey them again what is acceptable or not acceptable to you, and also that they can never harm you again....PAUSE 10 seconds..

That's right

Now you have defined your boundaries so let us return back to our peaceful meadow, free of the people who hurt you. You let go all your vengeance, anger, pain, fear in past. You will now loosen those people who hurt you and free up them. You can freely now explore new, healthy and trustworthy relationships in life. And the people who didn't apologize you will let them disappear.

Pause

The delicate moonlight is filling your meadow with magical healing light. Your younger self is sleeping freely to wake up on the new day of healing.

You are enjoying the moment of radiance. This radiance is comforting, soft and healing even more than you can imagine. All you can feel is light-hearted, free of all the anguish. Fear, anger, shame these are long gone from your life. Your heart and mind are stress-free and light, they are so light as if you can imagine yourself flying.

Pause

After all this, you realize that your life is completely changed and you are grateful. Now you can achieve all the happiness you deserve without any obstacles.

You recognize that the new sunrise will be a new beginning for your life that will make accessible all the positivity to you. The injured part is healing with every breath you are taking.

Pause

If the suggestions and ideas of this recording are adequate to you then you keep on breathing. The more you will listen to this recording the faster and quickly you will relax and heal.

As you keep visiting your meadow either by listening to this recording or just by closing your eyes the more confidence, serene, harmony will flow to your outer mind. You are a completely new human being who is happier, contented, subtle, and powerful , living in this wonderful world.

Pause

You are adored and cherished with every passing day as you heal more deeply your internal and external worlds become delightful.

Exploring Coping Strategies

And you can overcome this addiction of consuming excessive alcohol in your own way and in your own time and a part of you know knows exactly why you have it when you do not want to have it.

Your mind can explore whether it's a pattern of behaviour that has its roots in the past or whether it's just a coping mechanism to some other problem. And just how when you get a set of new clothes and change your wardrobe, you stop using the old clothes and perhaps discard them.

And, similarly, when you accept a new way of living, you discard the old way of living and this new life could be full of health, motivations, rewards, goals, accomplishments, success, love, and laughter,

Pause

All the positive change that you desire will be in line with the person you are, having a positive influence on yourself and the people around you. And, you will be a new person, a healthy and happy person as if you are wearing a new suit with an absolutely new makeover.

The time has come to take back control from the old part of you that was sticking with the old habit serving no purpose really.

Pause

Perhaps it served some purpose in the past and I would like to say thanks to that part of you which perhaps served some kind of purpose for your good, when perhaps you could not think of better ways to cope up with things you needed to cope up with. But, with me, you can explore many possibilities and new ways to live a healthier life and cope up with difficulties through better ways.

Pause

Some of the coping strategies that will help you in difficult situations are breathing exercises. Breathing always helps as it ground you and aligns your emotional and mental bodies. Every time you are stressed, simply take deep breaths and with every breath you take, you will feel much relaxed and calmer.

Take 7 to 10 deep breaths and you will be much more calmer.

Another coping strategy is to be mindful and involve all your five senses to bring your thoughts back to the present moment, without judging yourself.

Here, are some ways to do so...

Remember the 54321 technique, where at 5, you look at the five different things around you, 4 touch the four different things around you, 3, you listen to three different sounds or noises around you, at 2, you smell two different smells…it could be your natural body odour, a book lying near you, or anything you notice that may have a smell. 1, you taste one thing. When this happens, you involve all your five senses and bring your thoughts back to the present moment. This is especially useful when you are constantly worrying about future or nervous about something…and overwhelmed by the thoughts about future…

Pause

The next coping strategy is to say the serenity prayer and surrender everything to god and continue to trust the process of life.

Repeat after me three times :

Give me the serenity to accept the things I cannot change (**Pause**) the strength and courage to change the things I can (**Pause**)
and the wisdom to know the difference (**Pause**)

Pause

Give me the serenity to accept the things I cannot change (**Pause**) the strength and courage to change the things I can (**Pause**)
and the wisdom to know the difference (**Pause**)

Give me the serenity to accept the things I cannot change (**Pause**) the strength and courage to change the things I can (**Pause**)
and the wisdom to know the difference (**Pause**)

That's right.

Sleep Better

As you continue to relax and continue to listen to each word I say, you further drift deeper into a beautiful state of relaxation. And with this, you feel the sense of confidence that you will fall asleep easily and every time you decide to sleep.

Pause

As you are relaxed now, it is easier for you to fall asleep and every day when you relax yourself like this, you would easily and instantly fall into the deepest and restful slumber.

Deep relaxation is the prelude to the beautiful sleep and you inform your subconscious mind how much you desire to sleep better so that you wake up feeling fresh, alert, and happy.

And, as you continue to listen to each word I say, every word makes a powerful impact on your subconscious and allows it to do whatever healthy and powerful things it takes you to achieve your goal of sleeping fast and peacefully as soon as you lay on the bed with the goal to sleep and achieve a restful sleep.

Pause

And with each breath and every rise and fall of your chest, all these words and your thoughts about achieving a restful sleep get magnified and locked in your powerful subconscious mind.

You inform your subconscious mind the goal and why is it important for you to sleep on time.

Pause

The goal is to sleep fully and deeply without night time awakenings unless the nature calls so that you wake up feeling totally refreshed and energetic.

Your creative and powerful mind is listening to me and locking in these ideas to implement them when you are up and awake.

Pause

And, I am going to be taking to that part of you now about the first idea that will help you fall asleep easily. And, that sleep is natural and effortless. It is not to be tried, it is to be allowed. Every human and animal sleeps because it is natural. However, some of us may have difficulty falling asleep because we get confused between naturally sleeping and trying to sleep, and because trying requires an effort, and making an effort causes us to stay up.

Today is the day to understand this idea and implement it. From now on, you do not try but allow yourself to get completely relaxed and flow gently into the state of mind just how you are relaxed now to promote sleep.

And, I wonder if you could now imagine a beautiful garden, the garden you feel is safe and been to before. Or maybe, you want to imagine an absolutely new garden that is safe, secure, and beautiful to look at.

Pause (10 seconds)

And, as you imagine this beautiful garden, I would like you to look around and see the beautiful trees, the lush green grass, the colours of the sky and feel the pleasant breeze. Perhaps you can even smell the moss and the fresh air.

It looks beautiful around and you feel absolutely wonderful, isn't it?

Maybe some time ago, there was a part of you which became fearful of sleeping for whatever reasons or maybe you did not want to lose control and wanted to control sleep. The reasons could be many. And, perhaps that was the best solution you found to cope with something….the solution of not falling asleep. But this was long time ago and now you know the importance of sleeping every night.

Therefore, you allow yourself to let the past fade away….as if you are leaving everything behind you and entering a tunnel to a brighter and new side.

Pause

The new side is the new day where you begin to feel and think different about sleep. The new life where you sleep peacefully every night and wake up feeling fresh and energised the next morning.

I want you to imagine that now…

And, as you imagine this new day with a new beginning, you find yourself swinging in a hammock tied between two trees.

You allow yourself to completely relax as you enjoy each swing from right to left and left to right…

And you look at the Sun going down….and the birds chirping….and it starts to get dark around you….

Pause (10 seconds)

So, let's move into sleep, and as I say that, I mean you focus on breath and the rise and fall of your chest. And as you focus on the breath, you count yourself down from 20 down to 0, continuing to feel smooth and rhythmic breath you feel moving in through your nose and moving out of your mouth.

That's right…

And with each count down, you will drift into a deeper state of relaxation

20…..19……18…….17……..16…….15………14…………...13………12………11……drifting deeper and deeper….10…..9……8……7…..6……5…….4……3…….2……1…0…..

Pause

And this how you fall into a deep slumber every night….and every time you lay on the bed for the purpose of sleeping, you imagine this beautiful garden, the lush green garden with beautiful sky and find yourself in a hammock.

And as you swing in it, you begin to notice the rise and fall of your chest as you breathe and with every swing from left to right and right to left, you count down from 20 down to 0….and you will notice the sun going down and it goes down, you notice yourself drifting into a beautiful state of mind, which is deep and restful sleep.

Affirmations

1. You are getting healthier (7 seconds pause)
2. You breathe better and your health is getting better (7 seconds pause)
3. You love your body and you take utmost care of it (7 seconds pause)
4. You look forward to living an alcohol-free life (7 seconds pause)
5. You dislike the taste of alcohol (7 seconds pause)
6. Alcohol remind you of liver failure and all the costs that come with it (7 seconds pause)
7. You enjoy being sober (7 seconds pause)
8. You love yourself unconditionally (7 seconds pause)
9. You save money as a sober person (7 seconds pause)
10. You love yourself (7 seconds pause)
11. You love your body (7 seconds pause)
12. You want to live a long life (7 seconds pause)
13. You want to enjoy the gifts of life (7 seconds pause)
14. You drink 8 to 10 glasses of water everyday (7 seconds pause)
15. You take care of your health everyday (7 seconds pause)
16. You love to exercise (7 seconds pause)
17. You sleep on time and take care of your sleep cycle (7 seconds pause)
18. Your feel energetic as a sober (7 seconds pause)
19. Your skin glows with health and radiance (7 seconds pause)
20. You breathe fresh air (7 seconds pause)
21. You have more interesting things to do in life now (7 seconds pause)
22. You love all the time you have to be productive and to learn new things in life (7 seconds pause) (7 seconds pause)
23. You feel amazing as an individual (7 seconds pause)
24. Your self love and self-appreciation has increased (7 seconds pause)
25. You respect your body, mind, and soul (7 seconds pause)
26. Everyday, you are feeling healthier and happier (7 seconds pause)
27. You prefer to have soft drinks when you go out and socialise (7 seconds pause)
28. You choose to live as sober. (7 seconds pause)
29. You choose to not drink and feel great about yourself (7 seconds pause)
30. You live a beautiful life (7 seconds pause)
31. Your liver and other organs are feeling great with every passing day (7 seconds pause)
32. You love your family (7 seconds pause)
33. You have a deep love for your body (7 seconds pause)
34. Your self-esteem improves with every passing day (7 seconds pause)
35. Your health is improving with every passing day (7 seconds pause)
36. You are able to taste food better (7 seconds pause)
37. You are much calmer and relaxed (7 seconds pause)
38. Your relationships improve with every passing day completely (7 seconds pause)
39. You see a positive change in people around you (7 seconds pause)

40. You sleep better and fall asleep faster (7 seconds pause)
41. You have taken charge of your health and body and that makes you feel amazing (7 seconds pause)
42. You are happy and positive (7 seconds pause)
43. You are proud of yourself to have overcome alcohol addiction (7 seconds pause)
44. You are stronger than a hard drink (7 seconds pause)
45. You are the master of your mind (7 seconds pause)
46. You have control on your thoughts (7 seconds pause)
47. You are proud to have a healthy lifestyle (7 seconds pause)
48. You inspire people (7 seconds pause)
49. You breathe better (7 seconds pause)
50. You breathe fresh air (7 seconds pause)
51. You are stronger than any habit (7 seconds pause)
52. You can change habits easily (7 seconds pause)
53. You choose to live a healthy and happy life (7 seconds pause)
54. You overcome unhealthy habits easily (7 seconds pause)
55. You deserve an amazing life (7 seconds pause)
56. You are incredible and powerful (7 seconds pause)
57. You are positive and happier (7 seconds pause)
58. You are grateful for this change (7 seconds pause)
59. Alcohol dependency is a thing of past (7 seconds pause)
60. You relax yourself easily when you are stressed (7 seconds pause)
61. You manage stress easily (7 seconds pause)
62. You don't let anything affect your life (7 seconds pause)
63. You are living a beautiful and healthy life (7 seconds pause)
64. Life is all good and healthy now (7 seconds pause)
65. You love yourself a lot (7 seconds pause)
66. Life is beautiful (7 seconds pause)
67. You love your body (7 seconds pause)
68. Your health is most important for you (7 seconds pause)
69. You breathe fresh and clean air (7 seconds pause)
70. Your liver is getting healed (7 seconds pause)
71. Your body is your sacred place (7 seconds pause)
72. You love yourself (7 seconds pause)

73. You are full of vitality and energy (7 seconds pause)
74. You love to exercise because it makes you happy (7 seconds pause)
75. You are releasing weight effortlessly (7 seconds pause)
76. You are willing to change (7 seconds pause)
77. You let go of the past easily (7 seconds pause)
78. You are getting energetic with every passing day (7 seconds pause)
79. You pay attention to your sleep (7 seconds pause)
80. I am strong and healthy. (7 seconds pause)
81. You drink at least eight glasses of water everyday (7 seconds pause)
82. You look forward to your daily workout sessions. (7 seconds pause)
83. You listen to the signal and stop when you have eaten enough (7 seconds pause)
84. You are healthy and happy (7 seconds pause)

85. You love to exercise everyday (7 seconds pause)
86. You love to eat fruits and vegetables everyday (7 seconds pause)
87. You are becoming stronger and slimmer with every passing day (7 seconds pause)
88. When you crave sugar, you eat natural foods (7 seconds pause)
89. You are grateful for your health (7 seconds pause)
90. You are practice gratitude everyday (7 seconds pause)
91. You are open to new ways of eating (7 seconds pause)
92. You choose food that make your body stronger and healthier (7 seconds pause)
93. You chew food slowly (7 seconds pause)
94. You relish each mouthful and chew food at least 10 times (7 seconds pause)
95. You are becoming slimmer and lighter every day (7 seconds pause)
96. You love your body and mind (7 seconds pause)
97. You enjoy taking care of your body and mind (7 seconds pause)
98. You maintain sleep hygiene everyday (7 seconds pause)
99. You limit your day time naps to 30 minutes (7 seconds pause)
100. You can do it (7 seconds pause)
101. You are flexible (7 seconds pause)
102. You listen to your body (7 seconds pause)
103. You eat in moderation (7 seconds pause)
104. You eat wholesome foods (7 seconds pause)
105. You leave your past behind (7 seconds pause)
106. You feel decisive and enthusiastic (7 seconds pause)
107. You love your life (7 seconds pause)
108. You set everyday sleep and weight loss goals (7 seconds pause)
109. You take everyday actions to achieve goals (7 seconds pause)
110. You are motivated (7 seconds pause)
111. You focus on the good (7 seconds pause)
112. You are grateful (7 seconds pause)
113. You are happy (7 seconds pause)
114. You are self-aware (7 seconds pause)
115. pause)
116. .You see beauty in your body (7 seconds pause)
117. You learn new ways easily (7 seconds pause)
118. Your body is getting healed (7 seconds pause)
119. Every day you wake up you have feelings of gratitude (7 seconds pause)
120. You trust the process of life (7 seconds pause)
121. You trust yourself and trust your body (7 seconds pause)
122. You love yourself (7 seconds pause)
123. You are compassionate towards yourself (7 seconds pause)
124. You eat mindfully and enjoy every mouthful (7 seconds pause)
125. You are balanced (7 seconds pause)
126. You are competent and capable. (7 seconds pause)
127. You are worthy of love and care (7 seconds pause)
128. You give all the love and care to your own body first (7 seconds pause)
129. You choose positive thoughts (7 seconds pause)
130. You are blessed and abundant (7 seconds pause)
131. You love yourself unconditionally (7 seconds pause)
132. You are complete and whole. (7 seconds pause)
133. You are confident and courageous (7 seconds pause)

134. You forgive yourself for all the past mistakes (7 seconds pause)
135. You stay in present and are more mindful (7 seconds pause)
136. You are confident (7 seconds pause)
137. You have high self-esteem (7 seconds pause)
138. You are losing weight every day (7 seconds pause)
139. You are focused on your weight loss journey (7 seconds pause)
140. You pay attention to your food intake (7 seconds pause)
141. You love yourself unconditionally (7 seconds pause)
142. You are successful (7 seconds pause)
143. You are confident and motivated (7 seconds pause)
144. You believe in yourself (7 seconds pause)
145. You are good enough (7 seconds pause)
146. You enjoy healthy foods (7 seconds pause)
147. You do pleasurable activities everyday (7 seconds pause)
148. You are intelligent and wise (7 seconds pause)
149. You are lovable, open to receive and give love (7 seconds pause)
150. You enjoy your life and live it to the fullest (7 seconds pause)
151. You enjoy healthy food and drinks(7 seconds pause)
152. You have a beautiful relationship with food and your body (7 seconds pause)
153. You enjoy sleep and able to relax yourself easily (7 seconds pause)
154. You enjoy the process of self-hypnosis (7 seconds pause)
155. You enjoy being successful (7 seconds pause)
156. You inspire people by overcoming alcoholism (7 seconds pause)
157. You enjoy the benefits of being sober (7 seconds pause)
158. You imagine living a wonderful and long life as sober (7 seconds pause)
159. You spend more time with your family (7 seconds pause)
160. You let go of all the unhealthy habits (7 seconds pause)
161. You are success (7 seconds pause)
162. You are love (7 seconds pause)
163. You are happy (7 seconds pause)
164. You are positive (7 seconds pause)
165. You have high self-worth (7 seconds pause)
166. You enjoy living a quality life (7 seconds pause)
167. Life is wonderful (7 seconds pause)
168. You enjoy each day and live it to the fullest (7 seconds pause)
169. You are productive (7 seconds pause)
170. You are living a beautiful and healthy life now (7 seconds pause)
171. You hate the thought of drinking(7 seconds pause)
172. You enjoy every day (7 seconds pause)
173. You are a healthy and happy (7 seconds pause)
174. You are healthy and enjoy being healthy (7 seconds pause)
175. You keep your health on priority (7 seconds pause)
176. You enjoy all the benefits you see as sober (7 seconds pause)
177. You are loved (7 seconds pause) (7 seconds pause)
178. You are open to give and receive love (7 seconds pause)
179. You are in control (7 seconds pause)
180. You have high control on your habits and thoughts (7 seconds pause)
181. Your health is getting better with every passing day (7 seconds pause)
182. Your body is healing (7 seconds pause)

183. Your body is getting repaired from the alcohol (7 seconds pause)
184. You liver is getting healed (7 seconds pause)
185. You protect your inner child always (7 seconds pause)
186. You are whole and complete (7 seconds pause)
187. You love yourself unconditionally (7 seconds pause)
188. You are sober (7 seconds pause)
189. You take care of your health always (7 seconds pause)
190. You exercise regularly (7 seconds pause)
191. You eat healthy foods (7 seconds pause)
192. You enjoy the tastes of healthy foods (7 seconds pause)
193. Your sense of taste and smell is getting better with every passing day (7 seconds pause)
194. You listen to this recording regularly (7 seconds pause)
195. You are a healthy person and you inspire others (7 seconds pause)
196. You are assertive (7 seconds pause)
197. You easily say NO to alcohol (7 seconds pause)
198. You are an example for alcohol cessation (7 seconds pause)
199. You are the one who is in the driving seat of your life (7 seconds pause)
200. You are earning your right to live a sober life. (7 seconds pause)
201. You are forgiving yourself for what you did being influenced. (7 seconds pause)
202. Your life is getting unaffected by alcohol (7 seconds pause)
203. You can start finding the origin of your happiness within yourself. (7 seconds pause)
204. You are getting more powerful than your urges. (7 seconds pause)
205. You are having every reason to feel proud of yourself. (7 seconds pause)
206. You admire your physicality as well as your well-wishers. (7 seconds pause)
207. With each day, you are getting closer to the path of self-improvement. (7 seconds pause)
208. You are believing that you can get better (7 seconds pause)
209. You are becoming a better version of yourself. (7 seconds pause)
210. You are deserving of exceptional things in life (7 seconds pause)
211. You are loving the improvements in you as a person. (7 seconds pause)
212. Your loved ones love and adore you. (7 seconds pause)
213. You are becoming content with yourself (7 seconds pause)
214. You find your inner happiness with every passing day (7 seconds pause)
215. You are steadily taking charge of your own life (7 seconds pause)
216. You love and care for your body (7 seconds pause)
217. You have the power to face any hurdles that may come in your way. (7 seconds pause)
218. You have started mastering yourself to be in control. (7 seconds pause)
219. You surround yourself with supportive people (7 seconds pause)
220. You are gradually freeing yourself from your addiction to alcohol (7 seconds pause)
221. Each and every day you are getting closer to a life of being completely sober (7 seconds pause)
222. You are in charge of your life (7 seconds pause)

223. You forgive yourself for all the past mistakes done knowingly or unknowingly (7 seconds pause)
224. You have started a new life without the presence of any alcohol. (7 seconds pause)
225. With each passing day, you admire and love yourself more than before (7 seconds pause)
226. You surround yourself with healthy habits and come out as a strong individual. (7 seconds pause)
227. You have the power to reshape yourself into a more happier and peaceful person. (7 seconds pause)
228. You spend best time with the people in my life who are supportive and positive. (7 seconds pause)
229. It is natural that you are keeping yourself away from alcohol (7 seconds pause)
230. Life offers you great things and you deserve every bit of it. (7 seconds pause)
231. You are a happy and healthy individual and people start to notice it. (7 seconds pause)
232. With each passing day, your life is turning out to be better than before. (7 seconds pause)
233. You are worthy and free(7 seconds pause)
234. You have better relationships now (7 seconds pause)
235. People are finally seeing you as the one who overcomes his/her urges and habits (7 seconds pause)
236. Your body and spirit are on their way to the process of healing. (7 seconds pause)
237. Your life is eventually taking a turn for good once you set yourself free from alcohol addiction. (7 seconds pause)
238. Your choices define you and you are able to control them. (7 seconds pause)
239. You have the ability to have power over my urges to consume alcohol. (7 seconds pause)
240. You let yourself free and opt for a life without alcohol consumption. (7 seconds pause)
241. You motivate yourself to stop consuming alcohol altogether. (7 seconds pause). (7 seconds pause)
242. Your need for drinking alcohol is slowly getting released from your mind. (7 seconds pause)
243. You no longer have any impulse to drink alcohol. (7 seconds pause)
244. You don't crave for alcohol anymore as you don't find it enjoyable enough. (7 seconds pause)
245. Your life is meant to be enjoyed in many more ways other than having alcohol. (7 seconds pause)
246. You can free your life from the shackles of alcohol addiction. (7 seconds pause)
247. With each passing day, you are getting a hold on your alcohol addiction. (7 seconds pause)
248. You are getting closer to the life of sobriety with every day. (7 seconds pause)
249. You believe in yourself to quit drinking. (7 seconds pause)

250. You are bidding goodbye to your past and you are preparing to write your life's new chapter. (7 seconds pause)
251. Your relationship with people is healing along with your alcohol addiction. (7 seconds pause)
252. You deserve to lead a life full of peace and good health. (7 seconds pause)
253. You surround yourself with people who are there to love and support you. (7 seconds pause)
254. You have regained all the control in your life. (7 seconds pause)
255. One day at a time, you are starting to create your own reality. (7 seconds pause)
256. For all the choices you have made in the past, you are taking full responsibility. (7 seconds pause)
257. You are courageous and disciplined. (7 seconds pause)
258. You have gained power of self-control to relieve your life from alcohol addiction. (7 seconds pause)
259. You bring self-forgiveness into your life (7 seconds pause)
260. You become compassionate and loving towards yourself (7 seconds pause)
261. You take your commitments seriously. (7 seconds pause)
262. You are responsible. (7 seconds pause)
263. You dedicate your entire life to self-love and self-care. (7 seconds pause)
264. You learn to be more respectful toward your own body. (7 seconds pause)
265. You take care of yourself mentally, emotionally, and physically (7 seconds pause)
266. You prioritize your health more than anything. (7 seconds pause)
267. A healthy lifestyle is serving you the purpose to enjoy life even more. (7 seconds pause)
268. Every day your body is healing to become healthier. (7 seconds pause)
269. You adopt a new standard of a healthy lifestyle with this journey (7 seconds pause)
270. You enjoy the benefits of healthy habits in your life. (7 seconds pause)
271. You free yourself from everything that served you no purpose. (7 seconds pause)
272. Progression is much more important than perfection. (7 seconds pause)
273. You have the necessary faith in the process of recovery (7 seconds pause)
274. You are not going to let your past steal the thunder from your present. (7 seconds pause)
275. You are the caterpillar who thought the world was ending yet you chose to become the butterfly. (7 seconds pause)
276. The process of recovery is existing not for the ones who are in need but for the ones who want it. (7 seconds pause)
277. Recovery doesn't care about your mistakes rather it is emphasizing on lessons you are taking from your errors. (7 seconds pause)
278. Remember that growth comes from hardships and mistakes. (7 seconds pause)
279. Never go for choosing the path of excuses because it is nothing but the lies told by your own fear. (7 seconds pause)

280. You make your destiny when you allow your hardships to strengthen you. (7 seconds pause)
281. When you allow yourself to makes excuses then life makes it hard for you to excel at anything.
282. Start treat your willpower as your muscle. It gets stronger when you train it more often. (7 seconds pause)
283. All you need to do is keep going. When the time comes, everything will fall in place. (7 seconds pause)
284. Never get scared when you have to start over. Treating it like an opportunity where you can build yourself for the things you want can prove beneficial. (7 seconds pause)
285. Experience is a wonderful thing. (7 seconds pause)
286. Nobody said that it is going to be easy but it will be worth the struggle. (7 seconds pause)
287. Recovery doesn't get a day off. You keep working on it every single day for a fruitful outcome. (7 seconds pause)
288. Forgiving yourself to let go of your past mistakes. Forgiveness is another chance you can give it to yourself to start over. (7 seconds pause)
289. If you can go through the first day of quitting alcohol then you can do it for the lifetime. (7 seconds pause)
290. Your strength is not dependent on your psychical capacity rather it is arising from your power of determination. (7 seconds pause)
291. Through recovery, you are setting yourself free from your past by opening the gates of hell. (7 seconds pause)
292. Your own positive movie will be starting from the day when you have started living a sober life. (7 seconds pause)
293. Your strength is directly proportional to the things you are enduring after you're exhausted. (7 seconds pause)
294. it's time you made changes because you are the one who is holding yourself back from a beautiful life. (7 seconds pause)
295. When you strengthen yourself, you not only strengthen your body but also your confidence and self-esteem. (7 seconds pause)
296. Whenever you are denying alcohol in your life, your mind and body become more powerful. (7 seconds pause)
297. Refusing alcohol makes your mind is sharper than ever. It makes you more productive at what you do. (7 seconds pause)
298. You are well, safe, and secure (7 seconds pause)
299. You notice the positive impact of sobriety on your whole life. (7 seconds pause)
300. Everything in you life is gradually becoming better. (7 seconds pause)
301. You love the fact that you are not drinking anymore. Every aspect of life is good. (7 seconds pause)
302. You enjoy your life as a non-alcoholic. You are feeling good about yourself without the presence of alcohol in your life. (7 seconds pause)
303. Your life is great and fulfilling. (7 seconds pause)

304. You feel more than proud of your efforts to lead an alcohol-free life. (7 seconds pause)
305. Now that you have no alcohol in life, you are coming in contact with your fun and kind version of yourself. (7 seconds pause)
306. You have are finding your inner peace with every passing sober day. (7 seconds pause)
307. Being a non-drinker has made you speak more confidently and positively about your life. (7 seconds pause)
308. Your mind is getting clean and free from alcohol addiction. (7 seconds pause)
309. Now you have the will power to stay away from alcohol. (7 seconds pause)
310. With every day, you are feeling that your body is getting stronger and cleaner. (7 seconds pause)
311. You have gained control over your actions and it has helped me in making healthier lifestyle choices every day. (7 seconds pause)
312. You are strong and you are more than worthy of living a healthy life. (7 seconds pause)
313. Your body is clean and your choices have made your liver healthy again. (7 seconds pause)
314. You are entitled to keep all your organs in a stable condition. (7 seconds pause)
315. All your troubled thoughts are easily going away. Your are embracing positive habits in your life. (7 seconds pause)
316. Your heart, your nerves and your mind are getting better every day. (7 seconds pause)
317. You have opted for an alcohol-free life and it feels amazing. (7 seconds pause)
318. Now that you are away from alcohol, you will acquire a new sense of freedom in your life. (7 seconds pause)
319. With each new day, you are moving away from being alcoholic to a healthier and sober person. (7 seconds pause)
320. My nervous system and blood circulation is slowly getting better every day. (7 seconds pause)
321. Being a sober person, I no longer feel tensed in any situations. (7 seconds pause)
322. Now I can easily eliminate my urge to consume alcohol. (7 seconds pause)
323. Today I am a non-alcoholic person and I am overjoyed about it. (7 seconds pause)
324. It feels great to have clean and healthier body organs for a change. (7 seconds pause)
325. Now that I don't drink alcohol, I feel much more relaxed than ever. (7 seconds pause)
326. My body is on the recovery process in the best possible way. (7 seconds pause)
327. Every morning I wake up being satisfied with my choice of quitting alcohol. (7 seconds pause)
328. It was my choice to become a non-alcoholic being and I feel good about it. (7 seconds pause)

329. Once you choose the path of a sober person, you will start to love yourself even more. (7 seconds pause)
330. Quitting alcohol is easier than I have thought it would be. (7 seconds pause)
331. You have achieved nothing as a person who was addicted to alcohol. (7 seconds pause)
332. You can gain everything being a non-alcoholic person. (7 seconds pause)
333. Choosing a life that is not supported by alcohol is the best decision you'll ever make. (7 seconds pause)
334. Whenever I have the urge to drink, I breathe and dismiss those unhealthy thoughts. (7 seconds pause)
335. There is only exhausting hangovers and no genuine satisfaction from alcohol consumption. (7 seconds pause).
336. Time has come for you to free yourself from alcohol abuse. (7 seconds pause).
337. Now that I know myself better, I know the 'how' of quitting alcohol. (7 seconds pause).
338. You can master the art of quitting alcohol for life. (7 seconds pause).
339. You are glad that you left my days of alcohol abuse behind me. (7 seconds pause).
340. You will eventually be free from your addiction to alcohol. (7 seconds pause).
341. Meditation and long walks has made me found my inner peace. (7 seconds pause).
342. Your happiness is within you. (7 seconds pause).
343. You have to keep focusing on things that are positive in your life. (7 seconds pause).
344. Anxiety is no more a challenge and I am getting better every day. (7 seconds pause).
345. Being Calm and peaceful has become your forte. (7 seconds pause).
346. You make choices that will benefit you and your life. (7 seconds pause).
347. Once you take control of your habits, you can control of your life. (7 seconds pause).
348. Once your weakness is worn down, you will only grow with strength. (7 seconds pause).
349. Things that we repeatedly do define us and our lives. (7 seconds pause).
350. You need to maintain consistency in your life. Once you do that your habits will strengthen you. (7 seconds pause).
351. You can't stop until you reach the end of the finishing line. (7 seconds pause).
352. Attempting to live a sober life is nothing short of a marathon but I can finish it in one attempt. (7 seconds pause).
353. You can change your life by changing something you do it on a daily. (7 seconds pause).
354. You are loving the fact that your body is attaining its physical fitness. (7 seconds pause).
355. Every day your liver is healing from the alcohol abuses it faced over the past years. (7 seconds pause).

356. You get repelled over the thought of consuming even one drop of alcohol. (7 seconds pause).
357. You are happier and healthier. (7 seconds pause).
358. You are choosing your life over the sufferings that come from alcohol abuse. You are choosing a happy life over a depressed life. (7 seconds pause).
359. You are loving healthy food and you detest the presence of alcohol on your tongue. (7 seconds pause).
360. Your blood pressure isn't on higher levels anymore. All thanks to quitting alcohol. (7 seconds pause).
361. You know that you are loving yourself more than you love the toxic substance that is alcohol. (7 seconds pause).
362. You surrender yourself to the higher power (7 seconds pause).
363. You look forward to living a successful and fulfilling life (7 seconds pause).
364. You enjoy the present moment and eat healthy food (7 seconds pause).
365. You take care of your food intake and drinking habits (7 seconds pause).
366. You say NO every time you are offered drinks (7 seconds pause).
367. You know the amazing benefits of quitting alcohol (7 seconds pause).
368. You skin and your body feel amazing with every passing day (7 seconds pause).
369. It gets much easier to fall asleep (7 seconds pause).
370. You feel clean from inside (7 seconds pause).
371. People enjoy your company even more (7 seconds pause).
372. You inspire people and people look up to you (7 seconds pause).
373. You enjoy living a healthy life (7 seconds pause).
374. You love yourself fully and completely (7 seconds pause).
375. You love yourself unconditionally (7 seconds pause).
376. You like and admire yourself (7 seconds pause).
377. You are amazing (7 seconds pause).
378. You look and feel healthy (7 seconds pause).
379. People compliment you and you enjoy being healthy (7 seconds pause).
380. You look forward to living each day beautifully (7 seconds pause).
381. You are love (7 seconds pause).
382. You trust and respect yourself and your body (7 seconds pause).
383. You trust the process of life (7 seconds pause).

www.ingramcontent.com/pod-product-compliance
Lightning Source LLC
Chambersburg PA
CBHW081411080526
44589CB00016B/2526